DIRTY COLORS

Larissa Stawicki • Finn Bastian

DIRTY COLORS

Our adventure journal

and my declaration of love

to You, the PCT and Life

Hiked and written by

Larissa & Finn

Bibliographic information published by the Deutsche
Nationalbibliothek: Die Deutsche Nationalbibliothek lists
this publication in the Deutsche Nationalbiografie; detailed
bibliographic data are available on the internet: http://dnb.dnb.de

© 2022 Larissa Stawicki
Published and printed: BoD – Books on Demand,
Norderstedt

ISBN: 9783756860548

I wrote this book for

YOU · ME

OUR FAMILY · OUR FRIENDS

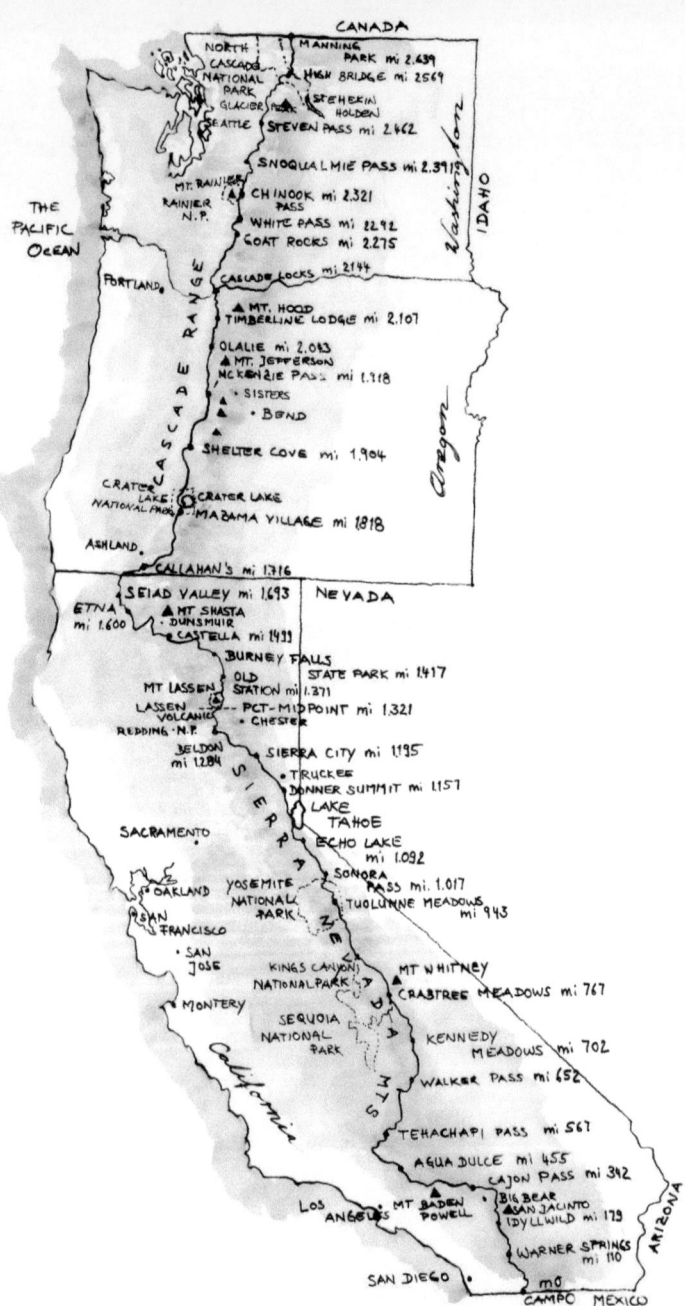

Contents

Prologue

About this book

"Hello."
"Hello, what can I do for you?"
"I'd like to refund this book please"

This wasn't about just any book! But a blue one, leather-like and with dotted pattern in the pages. I went back to the store just to exchange it for the blank-paged one I had bought ahead.

At this point, I had no idea I was about to experience my very first journey in which I'd actually end up writing an entire page every single day.

I started to write - and with every day I'd put down in my book, I stayed motivated to stay on top and not leave out a single day of memories. This is how my diary started and along the idea to turn it into a memorial book.

Finn and I were able to experience so many beautiful journeys together. We were to create memories that would shape and form our lives and that would nourish us in the future. Memories, that would cease to fade, as we have each other. Two people drawing all these beautiful moments from the treasure chest and reliving them together.

Perhaps this is why I never really cared to write a diary because I secretly knew, I would have you to dig up memories.

But in this case it somehow felt different. I managed to pick up the book every single evening to at least put down a few sentences. And a few times I'd trade in making dinner for you to finish my duty. Already back during our journey, we sometimes read from these memories to each other instead of our daily nightly television movie.

Ever since then I have become grateful for this daily evening routine. I'm happily allowing myself to sometimes be forgetful. And yet, it felt simple to put down these lines. I'd feel your presence - your essence inside of me. You manage to enliven my physical presence - playfully and somewhat magically enable me to write this book. Whereas it had been you, that was gifted to play with words.

And now, that your body has gone back to its roots, you are no longer able to assist me digging for memories. But instead I now have this book, we are having our story - bounded within a book.

You and I.

The essentials for my diary's content are thoughts, feelings, experiences and external forces that I would feel as I was writing. Those entries were written in the evenings in total exhaustion, shortly before I went to bed. They briefly reflect the days' occurrences.

One year ago, I started to add additional memories to the entries. Writing through the nights was a way of pulling through.

That's why I left the diary entries in their original versions and displayed them differently.

Enjoy the ride through an enchanting world that changes everything.

We ate like fat kids,

partied like rockstars

and looked like athletes.

We climbed mountains for breakfast

and beat the sun to the horizon.

We changed socks weekly

and our minds courageously.

We trusted our lives to strangers

and called them family.

We believed in magic

and often laughed at the moon.

- Quote from "The Hiker Yearbook, '19" -

An Epiphany to Take Form and Shape

It's 7 am, the sun slowly rises above the cities' roofs and sun rays start to tickle my eyes. I feel the warmth on my face, start to blink and close my eyes. I take a bite of my delicious bagel, feel the nutty taste of cheese on my tongue and dive into the morning's tranquility before the routine would get me going. A voice suddenly rips apart the cloud I am floating on and sits me back down on the chair.

"I want to hike the PCT."
Silence.

This thought must have been with you for a while now – perhaps you've even mentioned it and my ears were locked. Not responsive for this train of thought. So for me the idea was created at this very moment.

I didn't even have to ask which hike this was about. I was still all about my bagel when you delivered a short speech, summarizing all the relevant facts revolving this hike.

A hike to stretch from the Mexican all the way to the Canadian border, passing California, Oregon and Washington by foot – and where we'd have to be fully providing for ourselves. A hike to roughly take half a year and shoves some 149.175 meters of altitude difference up yours, which equals climbing the Mount Everest an easy sixteen times. A hike to make you carry your entire belongings on your back and to spend nights anywhere amongst rattle snakes, scorpions, bears and pumas. Pushing through desert, snow and rivers – miles away from any sort of civilization.

I'll be honest. I wasn't exactly thrilled. I chalked it off as a quickly fading idea of yours and put it off for later.

But the idea wouldn't just fade away. You kept bringing up the PCT (Pacific Crest Trail). You were trying to lure me into loving the idea. Using one of your powerful strengths, that is convincing and arguing in favor of your goals – almost leaving me no choice.

"I really don't feel like hiking. Why won't you just go by yourself, or why won't we simply turn it into a road trip?"

"We'll definitely do a road trip, but for now I want to hike, and that with you!"

"Let's graduate university first and then we'll see, alright?"

For the time being, this was my conclusion of the whole topic. Not for you though. You gathered information, dug deeper and ended up more consumed by the trail.

At this time, I was working together with Carsten who was

amidst building his company. Wanting to launch together with Franka and me. It was fun. Only two weeks prior we had signed the new contract. Then it really kicked off. I took a forced break from my studies for six months while waiting for my master's program. Every day I was at Carsten's office – when suddenly the message hit.

It was hard to grasp. You could infer that it was tough on him to find the proper words. A complete shock. He told Franka and me that he was diagnosed with a brain tumor, he'd have to give up on the office and wouldn't know how to proceed.

I cried. How could an amazing person like him at only 37 years old receive the message he'd only have one more year to live. I ceased to comprehend.

You caught my fall. Were there for me and provided me the strength I needed. I cried, looked into your eyes and said "I want to walk the PCT with you, when are we taking off? Let's take on the path and let's do it now!"

The coming weeks were some of the toughest ones in my life back then. Carsten was awaiting his surgery and – in case of him passing away – was to organize his office. Franka and I stayed in the office and supported him as much as possible.

He spent lots of time on the phone. Was talking to clients, companies and insurances. Repeating the particular sentence: "I have a brain tumor and will get surgery. If I die, I want everything to be in order."

I was so desperate, couldn't help myself and would cry every day. You were such a great support to me and had the biggest understanding.

Carsten talked a lot about his feelings and the letter he had written to his wife. He passed it to a friend and prepared everything for his death.

That was way too much for me to handle. How could a person gather so much strength and make the best of the situation.

I went through a time unlike anything I had ever gone through. It enriched me tremendously. I grew with it. Grew, like any living being that faces a challenge just to master it. You grow and learn. Earn experiences that will fuel you in the future.

Someone rings the door. It's the postman. He delivers a rolled up package for Finn Bastian, for you. It contains a map of the Pacific Crest Trail. The map is hung up. In the living room. We're actually doing it! We're telling everyone so we can't back out. You're buying a new backpack before we even remotely know what we are going to need. Telling me it's just to make sure we will do it for real. A "small" 45-liter backpack by Fjäll-räven. It's the "Abiko Friluft" model in dazzling orange colors.

Shortly afterwards we settle for a tent, sleeping peds, cooker, a second cooker (because one is not enough), pots, shoes, socks, bottles for water and a new backpack for myself.

We started doing rehearsal hikes. Three day hikes to be precise. Never before had we hiked. We would have to try it out eventually how hard it would actually be.

15 kilometers into the hike and I couldn't continue as some crazy pain went up from my Achilles' tendon all the way to my butt. During the second hike, I thought my shoulders were about to burst if I were to try putting my backpack back on. And after the third hike, I was unable to walk for several days.

We concluded: "It might turn out tough."

Nevertheless, it just pushed us more into the challenge. In this preparation phase we were entirely focused on making money which meant working through many weekends next to taking on our studies. We didn't watch a single video, avoided pictures and reports of the PCT in order not to be influenced. Wanting to make our very own experiences. We would have the first 700 miles as a preparation phase, as they would simply be through flat desert. Or so we thought.

And just like that, it was November. Permit-Day. Prior to taking on the complete hike, we would need a permit. The Pacific Crest Trail Association (PCTA) issues merely 50 permits every kick-off day as a measurement to keep the hikers' impact on nature as small as possible.

And thus, we found ourselves among over 4000 people in the virtual waiting line – with our faith in receiving the permit rapidly decreasing. To obtain a permit for the end of March seemed sheer impossible – especially for the both of us. And that's how the day ended – without the craved permit. In January, however, the PCTA issues a further set of permits. So we were forced to cancel our subtenants and were left hoping for air fares not to rise excessively throughout January. You kept saying you would be on your way either way – with or without the permit. But the issuing system does make sense to be taken seriously, and eventually we obtained our permit in January. 29 March in the year 2019 was the day for the both of us. The day was set in stone and just one hour later we booked our flights. 26 March we would be leaving and return 17 September. Due to my photographic skills we quickly found new subtenants.

After some initial issues, we also received our six-month visa.

We ticked off the whole list of doctors: Dentist, gynecologist, osteopath and our family doctor. The latter would recommend you to lose some 10kg before leaving in order to go be easy on your joints. Too bad Christmas was just around the corner and you wouldn't lose but actually gain 10kg. Your suit for my friend Katha's wedding turned out too tight and the gym most likely considered filing a missing person's report. But all that didn't matter because we were about to head into our great adventure.

22 March of 2019, Finn and Larissa have been a couple for nine years. We wanted to go to the cinema but couldn't make time. Didn't really matter as we had each other – as you phrased it. I totally got you, after a brief drama queen play of mine.

The day afterwards we threw a party. Everyone knew where we were headed. Naturally, because we'd tell everyone, just to ensure to ourselves we would be taking off for real. Perhaps fifty, sixty or even more friends came. We had an incredible night. Just like always when we'd get together with all our friends. Pure joy, exhilaration and the beautiful feeling of community – still, after all these years!

We landed in San Diego with high expectations for what lay ahead of us. Your aunt Elke, uncle Helge and your cousin Wynton picked us up and would show us a brief taste of Southern Californian lifestyle. We wined and dined wonderfully for some days and put on a few extra poundsies.

I started a diary.

Off to Adventure!

He starts to sing:

"Tell me somethin', girl
Are you happy in this modern world?
Or do you need more?
Is there somethin' else you're searchin' for?"

- "Shallow" by Lady Gaga & Bradley Cooper -

The whooshing pass of a train rips me from my thoughts. I close my eyes again, listen to the radio, hold your hand and there it is, her voice that in this very moment screams into me deep down:

The voice tags along:

"I'm off the deep end, watch as I dive in
I'll never meet the ground..."

- "Shallow" by Lady Gaga & Bradley Cooper -

Suddenly, I feel a tingling inside, my body is flooded with warmth and my heart is pounding a million miles an hour. The excitement and anticipation of the great adventure take over. What is awaiting us? Have we gone mad? Hold on, I can't take it! But the curiosity of the experiences we are to live beat every bit of anxiety.

There is a particular, short time-frame, in which you encounter yourself just before the adventure kicks off, where you could still retreat from it. As of tomorrow, you will be extracted from all your habits, your comfort zone, your daily routine and will have to bear the massive consequences evolving from that, leading into the journey of change.

The duet commences:

"In the shallow, shallow
In the shallow, shallow..."

- "Shallow" by Lady Gaga & Bradley Cooper -

Our excitement blows up like fireworks and merges with pure joy of life and thrives on the thirst to discover unknown lands. By now, there is full acceptance to walk new paths and to disconnect from the daily routine.

I feel goosebumps on my arms, a wide smile emerges on my face, my eyes still closed – I grab your hand and can't wait to move forward into the new chapter – by your side!

The flights were okay. I slept quite a lot and all the three (Elke, Helge & Wynton) were there to pick us up from the airport. In the first three days, they'd cover all our expenses and would take us out. So kind!

Unfortunately, I had gotten sick Thursday evening which delayed our leave by one day. I spent the entire Friday the 29 of March (originally scheduled day of permit) in bed while the others went out to get some delicious food. Sleeping through Friday did great! Hence, we could get going the next day, 30 March of 2019.

You had your little book as well. That you ceased to carry along already two weeks in. That one page you had written on got ripped out with its two entries. My task was clear, I'd proceed with the diary – challenge accepted!

Your entries can't be left out right now. They tell the story of us, how after nine years by your side, numerous journeys, experiences and life challenges we still were so different in some aspects. Your unshaken tranquility would sometimes drive me equally crazy and utterly envious. My sense for perfectionism would sometimes be in the way. On the other hand you were inspired by it and would drive you to finishing your assignments only a few hours ahead of the flight.

DAY 1   (YOUR ENTRY)

With Elke, Wynton and Helge from SD – kickoff. Car wouldn't crank. Took off around noon.
Distance of ~8 miles.

We all hit PCT Southern Terminus around 11:30am. It was very windy. The sun was shining and we were on our way pretty soon. The cold I had carried along constantly showed its presence! The nose was running and I had a headache. Unfortunately. After mile 8-9 we found a beautiful spot. The tent was mounted around 5:30pm, I took some aspirin, laid down and quickly felt better. While Finn was preparing dinner, a fellow hiker came by our "camp" – Ben. He camped just a quarter hour from us.

Early to bed and slept right away.

Ben, the first PCT-hiker we would be getting to know a little further the next days.

A skinny, e-cigarette smoking Australian in his early 30s with dark, longish hair. His story: He had already previously attempted walking the PCT. A few years back, there he was, at the Southern Terminus, the southern starting point of the hike. The sun was beating down, that year's optimal hiking season had already passed. He stood all by himself, as everyone else was already on their way. Just try it out, he was thinking. But the true beauty of the hike are the people. Those people, that already were ahead of him by a few hundred miles. Thus, he decided to be "flipping" from Warner Springs on. Catching up with the others and skipping the hike. However, he realized even if he ended the hike up in Canada, it hadn't really been a hike. So he cancelled the whole thing and left. And here he is, years later, to finish what had troubled him all the time.

Already the first few miles, encounters and conversations with fellow hikers showed us that we were part of a world on its own, we got to know the language of the hikers.

'Hiker Talk'. What the heck are you talking about?

Life on the trail is a closed-off world. The symbiotic lifestyle between nature and those humans, that walk the same path, share the same objective with you.

It wasn't that obvious in the beginning, but after a few hundred miles you notice people dropping out. Many cancel the journey, for they had imagined it differently. They had tried though – so hats off! Some simply want to walk a part of it, others are forced to return home for different reasons. Everyone to join this walk has his or her very own personal story. Sometimes they are told, sometimes it's all about the latest "shit in the woods". We are all in the same boat, as they say.

I always figured that we all together had chosen this very situation in which we deliberately fight for survival out here. We plan our isolation, would prepare for it every time we were to leave a town. Pack our bags with the calculated food we needed to reach the next city. Sometimes we calculated wrongly. Either way, it sucks: If you pack too much, you carry surplus food on your back all day every day, thinking "No more of the cereal bars please. Don't we have some more of the delicious chips?"

If you pack too little, you're running! You walk as fast as you can, sleep as little as possible and your breaks become super short in order to reach food in the quickest fashion. And they all know how you feel. Because everyone experiences this.

You get along, regardless whether you've been chatting a few minutes, passing to greet each other – or hiking together some days, weeks or even months.

This is how the trail shapes one language for all. A language to leave non-hikers in the dark.

It starts with different terms for different types of hikers for this long-distance-hike. If you manage to walk the entire PCT within one year by foot or ride by horse, you will be awarded "Thruhiker".

Some differences to note: There are the "Continuous-Foot-path" people meaning weirdos like Finn and I, that would walk back to the other side of the road, in case we had hitchhiked a few meters – absolutely ridiculous, just making sure to have walked every meter, inch, foot and whatever measurement there is. I do understand, however, if non-hikers do not understand.

Then there is "flip-flop", meaning a jump to a different position within the PCT, before returning to the initial point at later times. This occurs mainly due to weather conditions. And then there is "skipping", when hikers leave out entire passages, often times the High Sierra Nevada. Then you won't be considered a Thruhiker though.

Nevertheless, you shouldn't pay too much attention to these different terms as everyone goes their own way. Whether it's just a fraction, the whole path across different years or within a year. We all walk the path for ourselves and for nobody else. Thus, everyone decides for him- or herself how to handle the PCT. Whether it's northbound "NoBo", meaning to start from Mexico to reach Canada, or southbound "SoBo", that account for merely five percent of the hikers.

"But I want to walk southbound"

– "What does that mean?" I asked you when you were telling a little more about the PCT a year ago.

"That means hiking from Canada to Mexico. Which is more difficult, because your time frame is reduced and have way less hikers around you." – "Why, though? We have never hiked before and don't even know if we last a single week."

But you're just responding: "I don't want to be like everyone else!"

I can't remember how I convinced you to walk northbound. The time frame "NoBo" allows you seemed already very tight to me, and California's desert would come in handy as a "preparation".

So you kick it off in the desert. You should do so before the real summer hits and dries up natural water springs. You enter the High Sierra Nevada after 700 miles. A high-altitude mountain range to be covered in snow for the majority of the year. In June, snow starts melting away. They say you can enter the Sierra in a "low snow year" as of early June, during a "high snow year" not before early July.

Most people handle those 700 miles in one or two months which makes 15 April a popular starting date.

As soon as you leave the Sierra, you really have to crank it in order to reach the Canadian border before snowfall. This should be done before September. That is how the hike amounts to five or six months. This is the only yearly cycle where you can handle the PCT in a Thruhike. Those that leave southbound, can leave way later and hence have a shorter time frame before first snow hits the Sierra.

So, are we having a "low" or "high snow year"?

We witnessed some snow storms sweeping across the High Sierra right after our start, so we definitely had a beautiful year of snow.

Didn't matter that much, as we left without a hurry and were still in the process of getting used to the whole setting in the desert.

DAY 2   (YOUR ENTRY)

After an amazing sunset at the mountain where we had slept by ourselves, we left toward Hauser Creek. Went for a brief break to refill our water. Then started the "epic climb" toward Lake Morena. On arrival, we abstained from pizza but did take a sixpack of Budwiser to the camping ground. Tomorrow we will separate things!
(~12 miles)

DAY 2   03/31/2019   MILE ~ 8,5 - 20   (MY ENTRY)

We woke up with a beautiful sunrise and left around 8am.
15 minutes later we met Ben and hiked a bit together. It is tiring however, as you never know whether your pace is too fast or too slow ... At some point he wanted to repack his backpack so us two were on our own again.
We arrived at Hauser Creek at around 1pm to have a break and refill water. That was mile 15.4. Afterwards it was a

steep rise up to Lake Morena mile 20. We camped for 5$
each.

DAY 3   04/01/2019   MILE 20 - 32

We took off a little delayed to Boulder Oaks. There, we had a
two-hour break before continuing toward Fred Cayon. The
first one or two hours are always the worst for me. Afterwards, I get used to it. Tomorrow, we will try to leave a little
earlier (8am the latest) in order to avoid the heat.

DAY 4   04/02/2019   MILE 32 - 45   ~ 6.000 FT   MT. LAGUNA

Got going around 8:30am. Were having breakfast with the
dude and were sitting at the bonfire with his dog. Once
again, the first two hours were tough on me. The heat was
bearable thanks to a breeze. At 3:50pm sharp we arrived at
Mt. Lagunas's post office in order to send a few things back
to Helge & Elke.
Stocked up our food in the store around the corner and off
we went. Around 6/6:30pm it was a little late already and
we decided to mount the tent. Between some hills in a dip
because it's pretty stormy. Now we are worrying as some
rain is scheduled; some other hikers have their tents 100m
above us, where the wind blows way stronger. Perhaps we're
lucky and the rain won't pass our way. Or Karma will help
as we had given one of our spoons to the hiker with the dog
this very morning...
We shall see.

Note the fourth day's title above – "6.000 ft". By now we had realized that desert does not always equal the plains. There is a mountain range in this desert where we seem to be walking alongside, and up and down, respectively.

This is exactly why we hadn't sought information in advance. We wanted to experience each day in itself and not be influenced by others' pictures and reports.

Everyone writes their own history. Andrew, the photographer we met at mile 40, chose the task to gather some of those stories in an imagery book.

His project: One picture, one story. Many pictures, many stories. Bound together they form a book made up from many small personal stories covering the PCT hikers' experiences.

A snapshot of us let into our first trailmagic. Trailmagic, true magic, wizardry, a gift of truly unsolicited fortune!

An indescribable sensation getting to you when you pass a corner and unexpectedly see a group of hikers in the distance. Everyone equipped with a can of coke. You instantly know, trailmagic. The feeling of utter joy hits your stomach, you feel the unique tingling. You want to suppress that feeling as not to end up disappointed. Not noticing your walking pace is speeding up, your eyes locked on that billabong in the desert. Out of fear it will fade away, you're not daring to blink. Each step closer to it makes you realize it is for real. Your mouth shapes up to a big smile, radiating and reaching across your cheeks, you're running as tears are falling. You can't believe how fortunate you are. For days you had imagined the moment to sip an ice-cold drink when you're back in civilization. But so soon? You reach the cooler and see all these delicious, sugary drinks floating in water full of ice cubes. With your backpack still loaded, you reach in, open the can and take the first sip. A sparkle unfolds inside your mouth, all these wonderful small bubbles start to dance on your tongue and celebrate an experience of emotions, in order to prepare the rest of your body to this small but amazing symbiotic play of sugary liquid. The coke gushes down your throat slowly but in full ecstasy. Alongside with energy, that your body had been longing for days and now finally is replenished with. Goddamn that's one delicious coke!

You are in heaven, in Alice's Wonderland, in paradise, with parrots up in the sky, flooded with the sensation of joy so strong, that no pain, no hunger, no worry in the world would be able to take it from you. You are truly happy! Thankful to the person to have placed the cooling box. To the person ensuring that it is always filled with drinks. Thankful for this helpfulness.

The trail magic sometimes reaches unforeseen heights. People that sit down by the trail in their spare-time just to cook, prepare sandwiches and provide fresh fruits that you were missing for days. People that make us hikers more than happy by simply being part of this community. People we share our stories with. We call them the trail angels. True angels of the path!

Andrew as well handed us an ice cold coke, which definitely aided us in reaching the last miles before the post office.

DAY 5   04/03/2019   MILE 45 - 56

We barely slept. The wind started blowing crazy around 10pm. It blew above our tents, bounced off between the hills and touched our tent with an occasional breeze. But all remained intact and we were spared of rain. Later on we heard that in Mt. Laguna it really had been pouring down. Our Garmin's weather forecast had told us so as well, but gladly it was wrong.

We met Ben again when having a break and walked on with him. Shortly afterwards we hit a very steep and narrow path down. Honestly, was feeling a little uneasy...

Around 4:45pm we mounted our tent at a beautiful spot at mile ~56. Finn is already asleep :-)

DAY 6   04/04/2019   MILE 56 - 68

Today, we took of rather late and barely saw anyone else. The path went up and down and we reached a place to camp fairly early (I assume around 4/4:30pm). This was the first time we ran into another German hiker – Vanessa from Osnabrück. We sat down eating and chatting for a while. The views you get, when not looking down on where you're stepping, are breathtaking! We were already at 6.000 ft (according to my calculation some 2.000m).

DAY 7   04/05/2019   MILE 68 - 77

Great hike – up and down, we are advancing about 1 mile in half an hour. Now, that the heat is gone, hiking feels much lighter. But springs of water are becoming scarcer, too. Occasional water bottles were placed by "Trail Angels". You shouldn't rely on that, though, and you should always carry sufficient water with you. Today we marched nine miles straight and entered Julien together with two women by car.

We ordered pizza (18 inch) and for PCT hikers free apple pie.

Afterwards, Mark drove us back to the trail. It wasn't even on his way, he just couldn't stand the sight of us standing in the rain in Julien. Nice fellas all around! Laundry freshly done and a shower – now sand is blown into our faces...

Good night.

DAY 8   04/06/2019   MILE 77 - 87

Last night sucked so badly! Our spot at the RV park was super windy and dusty! We spent half the night keeping our tent in one place and ended up covered in sand.

We went back to the road quite late and 10 minutes into waiting were driven back to the trail by a sweet couple. I felt exhausted in the beginning until we encountered our first rattle snake. Finn was walking ahead of me as he suddenly noticed a rattling/swooshing noise 3-5 feet in front of him. He tried scaring it off with sand and stones – which worked just fine.

Shortly afterwards we met an older couple telling us about a rattle snake a little further down the road. We walked to-gether and – five minutes later – there it was, our second rattle snake. That one was silent though and Finn tried lur-ing it away again, but it remained in the bush less than a foot away from the path. The trouble was that on the one side of the path we had a steep cliff and on the other high mountains plus the snake. At some point Finn managed to pass and intended moving the snake with his hiking stick; but the couple and I didn't consider this the best idea – they were about to halt their hike but wanted to ensure our safe continuation. So Finn placed his backpack to block the bush and I could pass without being bitten.

We were done and took a break as the sun was nastily beating down on us. Some two hours later – the next shock – another one. That one was rattling again and even charged us. Finn's reaction was on point! Remained calmed and kept his eyes on her. Again, we had to chase it off somehow, as our option to the left was the steep cliff and the other part of the 2 feet track was pure rock. He again tried throwing small stones and sand – but this one was pissed and wouldn't budge from its charging position. Eventually it approached us but disappeared under a stone 2 feet from the path – giving us an ultimate rattling sound and leaving us in great relief ... (the rattling sound is somehow electric). About two hours later we reached a good spot to camp and were completely worn out by the day.

The feeling rushes through your whole body. It hits you like an electric pulse, unexpectedly and your body knows: Danger – freeze!

It moves so elegantly and gracile, wiggling forward fully loaded with muscles. It stands up and enters a charging position. Telling you: "One more step and I will inject you my poison, that will take you down."

Two weeks before in Germany, we had walked through nature in ease, barefoot with no danger around whatsoever – now to suddenly stay calm and not panic in this confrontation seems impossible.

But our original instinct is still there. You react naturally, remain calm. Adrenaline floods you, temporarily boosting your oxygen supply and pushing more oxygen to your cells. The bronchia widen, the heart beat increases and the level of insulin rises, as the liver cells are freeing up more glucose due to the adrenaline rush. Body functions unnecessary to the current situations are shut down. Required energy to boost your skills on short notice.

Where in our life are we still experiencing this? We live in a world covered in cotton wool. We no longer need the adrenaline. And yet, we experience it in our daily lives. When we are stressed out. When we are afraid. But when does it really save our lives?

Simply truly feeling your body again. Feeling nature. And learning to live with nature. The thrill to entirely rely on your instincts. You will be provided with that very sensation over there!

"I'm scared to be having nightmares tonight", I was telling you.

Had a fantastic night, slept roughly 12 hours and no wind this time. We got going at 9am when it was already super hot! No snake encounters and were provided water by the trailangels at mile 91. Each of us was carrying at least 3 liters of water in the backpack and we managed only to walk for seven more miles under a windless temperature of burning 35°C (95°F). Around 4:30pm we were some 3 miles from the next spring at a beautiful spot and will spend the night here.

"Horse" (Josh), a tall, ginger-headed hiker in his mid-thirties. Blue basketball pants, light-blue longsleeves and the hood always up, merely the sunglasses popping out, framed by a fully-grown beard.

Always in a good mood, resulting in a constant smile.

On our eighth day he passes us with big steps, shortly before our encounter with the third rattle snake. He is followed by a cloud of dust and I'm relieved we now have someone chasing off the snakes ahead of us.

It didn't work out just like that but later on at a dried-up stream where we mount our tent for the night behind a bush we meet him again.

He joins us and presents himself.

You are instantly in love with his "Hilleberg" tent, which we also had considered for us.

Horse tells us he had just finished another long-distance hike, called TA, down south in New Zealand which is why he now is in great shape.

He offers us to smoke a joint, but we – or rather I – thankfully refuse.

And with that he is gone for a few days, until we meet again along with other new faces up in San Jacinto Peak.

Yet another windless night. Early into the evening we saw coyotes about 30-50m (90-150ft) from our tent and got up with an alarm clock at 6am this time and left around 7:30am. Firstly, three miles to the next water spot, had breakfast over there, refilled water and left toward Warner Springs in an infernal heat. We were received with love, approx. 50 hikers are here... Taking shower, doing laundry, fixing up wounds, recharging electronic stuff, making phone calls and are improving their equipment in the "outfitter-van" – just like us; 340$ were spent on: A sleeping bag liner, crampons, a water bag, tape, electrolyte.

The school across offers food for 7$. So sweet.

We've decided to do a "zero-day".

Did a "zero-day" in Warner Springs, called mom and dad, had a shower (bucket-shower), did laundry and shopped for new food ... should be set to reach Idyllwild. Tomorrow morning we march on.

Zero-day. What does that mean? Walking not a single mile of the PCT. The most beautiful part of it is to consciously decide on this. "Resting" for one day. I'll explain the quotation marks shortly. Sometimes, however, you are having unsolicited zeros, that you can't fully enjoy. Days, where you procrastinate the hike so much that eventually it won't be worth it. So you are left with a guilty conscience because the next day you will have to make up for the lost miles.

But now I'm ahead of the story. This was long before that phase kicking in at mile 109. For now, it's all chill.

Even a zero might not what it seems, though. You try to sleep in, but anyone who has spent a night in a tent during summer knows that sleeping in is not that simple. Doesn't matter because everyone else is already up anyway, especially those that plan to leave today. So up we get and whilst having a cereal bar or sandwich checking in on the others. Ideally, the electric stuff has been charged through the night and the WiFi was activated. Checking the savings balance to see if we can continue the journey and quickly responded last week's 100 messages.

Where is the next laundromat and who wants to attend doing groceries in town. Are we walking? No way! After all we have walked enough and it's called zero-day for a reason and not "let's-walk-a-few-miles-to-the-supermarket-day". Often times there are trail angels giving you a ride or you use public transport.

Quickly putting on the rain coat and pants – not because it is raining or you wouldn't find anything more suitable to match the 35°C, but because you want to wash everything else (that one pair of long pants, three shorts, three pairs of underwear, two pairs of socks and two t-shirts). Ahead of doing groceries it's usually about having a burger with fries in order not to buy too much and eventually throw half of it into the "hikerbox".

Beer and delicious food in the evening.

Had a nice breakfast at the golf club and left around 11am.
First, we hiked through blossoming fields of flowers and
then passed along a beautiful creek. Further up the path
we mounted our tent and witnessed a stunning sunset and
found out, how we could attach our sleeping bags to each
other. This night we should not be freezing

Last night we were at a beautiful spot again with some fellas
called Don "Agent Orange", Ben "Dice-Man", Austin and
Chad.
Finn and I took off already at 8am and met the others for
lunch at Mikes Place. A fucked up location with total weirdos. No idea, whether Mike was there ... Anyway, all the
dudes were completely plastered.
After two hours we went on for another four miles.

This day was pretty good!
Left around 8am and chalked off 5 miles after only 2 hours,
refilled water at the creek and had oatmeal.
It had been our plan to hike 15-16 miles today, until we
met Chad at the creek. He told us that Ben was about to try
making it all the way to Paradise Valley (another 16 miles).

We did mile after mile without any major breaks (peeing breaks the most).

After some 15 miles my feet and knees started hurting. Upwards was still doable, but walking downwards was pure hell. The restaurant and delicious burgers that we were about to get our hands on kept me going. It felt like crossing 100 mountains (actually 5 or 6) before we finally reached P.V. and the burger was indeed pretty good! Best thing was ... we're allowed to sleep in the restaurant ... sooo nicely warm!

Also, we met the mayor of Idyllwild ... which is a dog ...

DAY 15   04/13/2019   MILE 152 - 160

At 7am everyone had their things ready and shortly after 8am the road house was packed. We had a chill breakfast and didn't wait for Ben "The Dice-Man". (To his bad luck he had mounted his tent too early and hence didn't sleep inside the café). Left around 11am and reached a nice camping location after a few breaks, as the sun was burning again.

DAY 16   04/14/2019   MILE 160 - 171

Today was the first time we'd use those crampons. We were facing a patch of snow of around 100m (300 ft). Ben had taken pictures ;-) In totally we did 13 miles today, because we went an additional mile to go down Cedar Spring to refill our water and another mile back up. At 7.000 ft we set up the tent.

That is where we are meeting the "Flying Dutchman", as Ben was calling him and his daughter. Another few hikers are camping at this location since its pure cliffs miles before and afterwards, making this the last possible spot to place your tent.

I am recalling all those many moments in which we were to make a decision whether to install our tent or to keep hiking, possibly risking to not be finding a usable spot for another two or even three hours.

Obviously, the map guiding you won't show you what it is actually like – whether it's all bushes and shrubs or even a cliff. The "half-mile-map" created by a fellow hiker was way more useful instead. It displays many camping spots and even estimates numbers of tents thereof. But again, you wouldn't know how many hikers were currently occupying the given locations.

Once you find a spot, it's that same procedure: Mounting the tent, blowing up the mattress, getting out the sleeping bag, installing the cooker, pouring water into the pot and off we go. The stomach rumbles and you look down your food bag. Is it two small packs of "ramen noodles" or mashed potatoes, already coming out of your ears by merely thinking of it – or will you treat yourself the one "Mountain-House-Meal" that you scheduled for this stretch?

"I can't handle mashed potatoes anymore and I will keep the delicious Pad Thai for a particularly tough day". That's how you make decisions every night, that have been with you since noon.

"So, do you already know what you'll have for dinner?", you're asking me every afternoon. "Probably ramen and I'll add a spoon of mashed potatoes as to thicken the water and definitely a spoon of peanut butter. Do we still have enough chips?

I'll add them in the end so they won't turn all soggy."

Your mouth is watering and you can't expect to finally eat some. At the same time you are fully aware it won't be sufficient food! It's just too many days ahead as if you were able to eat as much as you'd like to.

Discipline all around.

DAY 17   04/15/2019   MILE 171 - 179   (+2 MILES DEVIL SLIDE)

We mastered the first snow, it was a little sketchy. As Finn likes to put it: Always three points of contact! From mile 174 on, 90% of the hike was covered in snow all the way up to "Saddle Junction" ... easy! I fell on my butt twice but it was all good. From Saddle Junction on it was 2 miles to the car park and 20 minutes later we hitch hiked on the back of a pickup. At the camp in Idyllwild we met Ben again. Went to get food with "Sherlock". Veggie burgers.

My first hiking experience in snow. You and I, we had never worried about snow – being from cold, Northern Germany. As opposed to other hikers at the PCT, we do know what snow is all about. Couldn't be that different than going for a stroll in a snow-covered forest back home.

Or so we thought. But here we are. To the left, there is a steep cliff reaching up in a 90° angle. Icy parts here and there. An uneven path as narrow as a little over one foot. At times you are having to hop over a fallen tree. When you're turning to the right, you are stunned by the magnificent view across endless nature. You're able to be presented with this view because there is nothing beneath you for a few thousand feet. It's all the way down to your right, like a really far way down.

I try to maintain my view straight up, avoid looking down too much. Focused not to do a fatal step, always close behind you. Your feet are somewhat pulling me, calming me down.

And suddenly it's all white. Snow. Ice. The rocky path turns into a snowy path amid a huge area of snow. Keep going? Turn around? Crampon time!

"If we were to slip and slide, we can only hope for a tree to catch us on the first meters – without smashing our head first"

My thoughts are running wild. I let you go first, so I know you've made it. I've always been more scared about you than the other way round. I don't want to lose you. Love you too much. I couldn't take the pain. I'm sure.

We made it. Pure relief. Conclusion: I had no idea what was expecting us. Vertigo teaming up with snow. Perfect.

Keep on!

DAY 18   04/16/2019   ZERO-DAY   IDYLLWILD

Had our second zero-day. In Idyllwild. Did laundry first, then had burrito at "Lumber Mill", did groceries for the next eight days and then tried fitting everything into the stuff sacks. Equipped with a few beers and chips we went down to "Hot Food" and "Skippy Skunk" in their van, where Chad is also sleeping. Later on we had another veggie burger at "Lumber Mill".

It was drizzling half the day. Let's hope the mountain won't be covered in too much new snow.

It felt like 100 miles (2 miles in reality) passing the Devil Slide up to Saddle Junction. Instead of staying on the PCT, we moved toward San Jacinto Peak. Snow eventually did hit us again and it was crampons time again. From Saddle Junction up the peak it were supposed to be only 5.5 miles. In the end, it took us 5.5 hours to end up on top. Last section till the "Emergency Hut" was quite steep, so we'd feel a little uneasy. Once we made it to the hut, it were another half a mile up to the peak (we had left the backpacks at the hut). Half an hour later we had a breathtaking sunset with a 360° view across Southern California. Ten other guys stayed at the hut for the night.

The desert beneath our feet, the mountain shadows lie upon it and everyone stares intensely at the setting sun, leaving the horizon. We met "Feathers", "Sunshine", Zach, Alice and also "Horse" up the Peak.

"Feathers" (Kate) has got tattoos. Her trail name is also part of her ink, as a memorable trait for her passion to collect feathers to keep on her body. A skinny face, framed by long, dark blond hair usually up in braids. She rarely uses as cap, has sunglasses and a pink skirt that she swaps for "Long Johns" by night. Since she lacks her right clavicle, her "Z-Pack-Ultralight-Backpack" is basically only supported by one shoulder. This is no reason for her not to smile.

She shares her adventures with her YouTube followers in a particularly high-pitched voice and has since gained fair recognition.

She is a recent young mother to a daughter and now lives her dream to be free and independent.

We'd usually meet "Feathers" in the towns of Southern California. We kicked off our common adventure in High Sierra until at some point we lost track of her. More to this story later on.

"Sunshine" (Eric) is a highly social friend that loves to give a helping hand. We meet him as his head is covered in millions of curly hairs reaching all the way over his ears. A beard as dark as his curly-haired head and a light blue hoodie that tries to tame the vivid hair. In the cold mornings he wears functional leggings beneath his shorts in which he can't hide his "O-shaped-soccer-legs". Thanks to his German grandmother he knew some German and was glad to be practicing with us every now and then.

"Good job everyone", he'd always say to cheer us up. This man in his early twenties actually managed to inspire us all with his joyful spirit. Very mature in his approach, way more than many hikers who biologically were way older than him.

It was for this very reason that he was known under his trail name "Sunshine" – a name, he liked to adjust to all means on the trail: "Snowshine", "Sandshine", "Iceshine", "Rainshine", "Moonshine".

Since you were so much into computer science, you shared your idea of a PCT-communications-app. You'd spend days talking to "Sunshine" all about it. The idea of bringing people together – connecting them. During and also after the hike.

You created a mind map and suddenly there was even a board game. "Auf Achse" [German board game, engl.: "On the road"] but for hikers.

After the Sierra, he was also gone. He'd try keeping up with us. But were on a schedule and hence "Sunshine" ended up lagging behind a few days.

And then there was Zach on top of San Jacinto. You were fascinated by him right away. His style to take pictures – with his camera always ready. At this point, I don't even have to mention his beard and messy darkened hair cut – like almost every other male hiker. A rather quiet but very likable person. He took pictures of us. That one picture with the mountain's shadow in the back and us in the front. He caught the moment for all eternity, not only in the picture.

We truly got to know Alice and "Horse" only later on.

DAY 20   04/18/2019   MILE 190   SAN JACINTO PEAK

After a cold, sleepless night up in San Jacinto Peak, we watched a beautiful sunset at an altitude of 10.834 ft. We left the peak at around 7:30am and fought our way through deep snow. Two hours passed before we were back on the PCT which equaled 2.5 miles. Shortly into the PCT, we had a long break and Finn reclaimed the lack of sleep.

At noon, we slowly but surely marched on and the sun would partially melt the snow so much, that Finn at times would sink in all the way to his waist! Too bad for his shoes and feet. We arrived at a neat forest glade at 5:30pm, melted snow over the camp fire and met many other hikers, amongst which we met "Number 1", another German who'd been issued number one at the permit.

DAY 21   04/19/2019   MILE 190 - 205

We left in snow and arrived in the desert. Demounted the tent at 7.749 ft and put it back up at 1.744 ft. Crossed 6.000 ft in 8 hours ... and in between ... encountered nine snakes. The first one pretty early ... it was rattling as Finn was passing the bushes but we were unable to make it out. There was none in sight on the path either, so we quickly got going. Finn (he usually takes the lead) saw the second one sneak away leaving him without a sight of it ...I'm rushing by quickly again...no rattling. Finn completed missed out on the third one, whose "butt" was basically half way into the path. I halted right next to it on discovery (I was always 9 ft behind Finn during "Snake Lands") and backed up a few steps. We drove it away with sand toward the cliff. Number four and five were curled up in disguise right next to the way. They were rather young, without rattling sounds, and we only witnessed them because we stopped to have a sip. Then there were three "racer" snakes (black, very fast snakes with a stripes-pattern) and a very small one almost accidentally crushed by Finn.

It is full moon tonight and many are doing a "Full-Moon-Hike", we are watching the moon in awe from our tent, as he rises over the mountain.

Side note: First blister (heel).

After demounting our tent this morning, a fierce wind kicked in. "Perfect timing" we figured ...

Wind force increased and blew up the desert's sand. Shortly ahead of the Interstate 10 we reached a dry creek river bed and were absolutely "sandblasted". We advanced merely step by step, gathering forces against the wall of wind and sand shooting at us. Four miles into the hike that morning, we managed to reach a place beneath a breath of Interstate 10 and had our prayers heard when seeing "trail magic" right there. With a coke, an apple, an orange and some cereal bars we marched on. At the "Mensa Windmill Farm" we had a break from wind and sun, before continuing towards the Whitewater River. At times, the wind was so strong that I could barely stay on track which was quite scary considering the steep cliff. The plan was to reach Big Bear Lake but food has become scarce forcing us to leave track at Big Bear City. Sidenote: Second blister. The other heel.

We won't need to count Finn's blisters, we're just happy his toes are somewhat alive.

It was beneath the Interstate 10 that we met "Grumpy Bear" (Tyler) and "Snack Pack" (Jaroslava) for the very first time. Both are with Benny "The Diceman", as he was named on his first try on the PCT. The blasting wind is loaded with sand busting around their heads.

Long brown dread locks are kept with a buff out of her face, tanned and sporting some slick tattoos, wearing blue shorts, bleached up through the beating sun. (Later on I would have a pair of those shorts and keep wearing them with pleasure until this very day).

She introduces herself as Jaja and I'm guessing to spot a French accent.

Tyler from Canada is by her side. Longish, messy, black hair, like every other dude on this track, sunglasses and a blue shirt – Ben introduced him.

Those three are about to hitch a ride in order to get some grub from Subways, and we are off to marching some miles, so our encounter is of rather brief nature.

Later on, we'd meet again and walk a few miles the five of us together.

DAY 23   04/21/2019   MILE 220 - 235

We chalked off the first and possibly biggest water crossing in Southern California after about one mile.

After six miles, we had done several dozens of river crossings and I for the first time I put my sandals to good use. In the beginning, Finn would try to use stones and tree trunks to cross in a dry fashion but eventually rendered himself wetting his shoes. At some point, like the 20th river crossing, he stepped through in his Crocs. We had a longer lunch break, washed ourselves and did laundry in the river.

It was tough to keep track of the path within all these river crossings, which cost us major time. We had wanted to do 17 miles today, but managed a "mere" 15.5 miles (also due to hunger). Witnessed three snacks (1 rattle, 1 racer, 1 gophra).

The morning's ascent somewhat sucked this morning. After we kept pushing to somewhere less steep, we ultimately did manage to get into the "flow".

We crested three "mountains" (reaching even 8.700 ft) and back down to 7.400 ft. In between there was hail hitting us for about an hour, but we walked those 20 miles very smoothly. No further blisters. Finn's small toe is hurting and as of mile 12 it's always my feet, knees and occasionally the hip ending up a pain ...

But today it was ten times better than day 14. Tonight it's Arrastre Trail Camp with some 25 other hikers.

Hunger. Moisture. The cold. It all adds up this evening.

We marched so far, had sped up the pace to reach Big Bear one day early as we are left with almost no food. We're hungry, thirsty and are drenched by rain and hail. Shortly before we reach the camping spot, I felt like accidentally stepping into a mud-ridden puddle and got my shoes all wet. It sucks so badly, but we all share the same feelings and maximize the fun.

The first sip of a cold coke, the first bite of a burger and the feeling of fresh clothing on a showered body.

But not tonight. Tonight it's bedding all wet. The grey sky embraces our tents. The wind shoves fully blown water drops off the leaves and onto us as the daylight fades on the horizon. It's getting chilly and the wet backpacks fill the tent's interior with a humidity to announce a terribly cold sleepless night. We connected our sleeping bags, filled the Nalgene bottle with hot water and try to maintain our though of the next day's hot shower.

You lay there awake, the whole body shivers. Keep turning around, trying to get comfortable, you really can't though and just hope for tomorrow to come quickly before eventually falling asleep.

"Thanks mate", you're saying as you hide a few bucks in the car. You're opening the trunk to get our backpacks – hatch is closed and a salute to leave.

Here we are, not knowing where to go – and our stomachs are rumbling.

First off to the supermarket, turning on WiFi and browsing for a place to stay.

The store's selection is overwhelming, a true overkill for the eyes and the shopping cart appears too small to satisfy my stomach.

"How about potatoes with pasta, rice, enriched with a creamy spinach sauce, mushrooms, tomatoes, zucchini, garlic, and for dinner we'll have fruit salad with ice cream? And let's grab the 12-pack of donuts for everyone!"

"Let's take two instead, they're just three dollars each".

My mouth is watering and I'm gorging the first donut before we even leave the store.

An explosion of happy feels unleashed inside. I proceed to the second donut at once.

Letting your appetite run down the shopping list and cooking with friends. Talking in beautiful company and with full mouths about the PCT. Letting current events run down your mind again and planning the next steps. Or just staying silent while simply enjoying the culinary variety in your mouth. Appreciating what we have. Appreciating that we can be here and appreciating that we are in good health.

I awake, it's the next morning and a beautiful dream comes to an end.

"Hiker-hunger"!

DAY 25   04/23/2019   MILE 256 - 266   BIG BEAR LAKE

The night was rather frosty! It was so cold and moist. We just slept for a few hours and got up going already at 7:30am to get warm quickly. Three miles into the hike we refilled water and had our (almost) last food for breakfast. Very unfortunately did I slip when getting water, leaving my shoes completely soaked. To the disliking of my feet, I took on the last 7-8 miles in my sandals. We arrived around 2pm at Big Bear Lake (shared an Uber) and accidentally ran into "Sir Loin" (Ben), Tylor and Marguerite with whom we shared an AirBnb for the night. This night we'd definitely not be cold! Jaja and Parker, too, are with us in the house and tomorrow both of Marguerite's sisters will join us.

DAY 26   04/24/2019   ZERO-DAY   BIG BEAR LAKE

Breakfast, re-supply, and back to the AirBnb by bus. Had a foot-bath and a super delicious BBQ with veggie burgers. The hikers are: Jaja (Czech Republic), Ben "Sir Loin" (Aussi), Tylor (Canada), Parker (US), Marguerite, Alice & Alexa, Lulu, "Sunshine", Zach.
And there was Margarita as well ... delicious ...

We got to know the three sisters up here in Big Bear Lake. "Hop Along" (Marguerite), "Master Braider" (Alice) and Alexa. Marguerite and Alice are twins and both beauteous, curly hair whereas Alexa has long, straight hair.

The three sisters wouldn't always hike together. Marguerite was lagging behind due to her foot injury and therefore skipped a few passages. Also Alexa joined in at a later point in time. But wherever the three sisters unite, they communicate in their secret language their grandmother had once passed onto them.

It was also the "five-star-poop" the sisters would teach us:

*Scenery	A fantastic view.
*Cat hole	Great soil to dig a deep hole.
*Perfect squat	The perfect seat, ideally a fallen trunk (medieval style)
*Wildlife	Enriching time through watching animals
*Ghost wipe	The infamous, surplus piece of toilet paper

Then there was Lulu from France and Parker from Michigan. We met Lulu only for a few times but we got to know Parker pretty well.

He has – I'm having to repeat myself once again – messy, medium long blond hair, lapping out of his cap. His cap, the very same as mine, features a bear by "Patagonia". Parker is a carpenter and thus had many options for a trail name.

„Wow, take a look at this beautiful handicraft on that door frame."

He randomly shouted out his thoughts, slicing through our

conversation, starring at the AirBnb's terrace door. We started laughing and "Sir Loin" comes up with "Parquetry".

"That's perfect". Tyler is thrilled.

"Oh no, I know a much better name for Parker!", interrupts "Snack Pack" with enthusiastic laughter.

"Don't you remember the story he told us a few days ago? His name should be: 'Vibrate'". She laughs and suddenly everyone is in silence.

"What story?", are you asking and start to smirk.

"No, that's super embarrassing"."

"C'mon man, now you have to tell us", are we teasing.

"Fine", Parker starts chuckling and dives back into that moment.

„I was hiking very late that day and really needed a camp spot. Finally I found a good one for me. Just a small one but perfect for my tent. Just before I finished setting up, a girl came along and asked if she could join. I made some room and she set up her tent right next to mine. It was already dark and we went to bed without talking at all. If I would have been her I probably wouldn't camp next to a stranger all by myself. But anyway I just wanted to get the last things out of my backpack and then it happened. Suddenly I heard this noise like a vibrator. I thought 'Shit, what's she doing there' and couldn't stop giggling. After a while I realized it wasn't in her tent. This vibration came out of my backpack. I panicked. Rapidly I tried to find the source. I already knew it must be my shaver. I was so embarrassed and it took so long to find this fucking thing. Finally I found it and turned it off. I was bright red and she, silent. Next morning she was gone before I was awake. I hope I will never meet her again."

You've always really liked Parker! Were always happy when

knowing he was in town. Or when the group caught up with us in the Sierra and we'd cross the mountains together. Alice as well likes him, and he likes her ...

DAY 27   04/25/2019   MILE 266 - 275

Today we only managed to leave at 1pm. Had breakfast at "Copper Q" and had a fine fruit salad back at the house. An Uber dropped as at the trail head. Backpacks heavy as led but thankfully it wasn't all steep up. A small baby rattle snake crossed our path and Tylor claims he found bearish excrements.
Let's see if we'll have a visit tonight.

DAY 28   04/26/2019   MILE 275 - 292

We slept well, not too cold and no unsolicited visits. Today, lots of downhill. Solid 17 miles to the camping spot. We had a nice siesta and Finn almost got jumped by a racer. And we had freshly baked pumpkin-banana-bread by Mark and Vikki, who coincidentally know some people back in Eckernförde.

DAY 29   04/27/2019   MILE 292 - 308

Today was an exhausting yet beautiful day!
I tripped and fell three times but no major harm each time. I could cool down my foot right away twice at the river. We went bathing at "Deep Creek" where we met some locals that even offered us a sandwich...

Which was amazing! Definitely my highlight of the day. To-day, Finn once more was surprised by a racer snake – actu-ally the other way round, and the snake quickly fled into the tree. The "deep creek" paved our entire way all along and we had a constant stunning view! Finally, we reach the Hot Pools. Many youngsters enjoying their weekends down here. Tomorrow we'll enter the pools.

DAY 30   04/28/2019   MILE 308 - 328

The pools were great! Finn got up super early like at 6am and jumped into one of the hot pools. I followed briefly af-terwards. We got going only around 8:45am when it was al-ready burning hot. Our goal was to reach the Picknick Area about 18 miles away. Today's trail was quite alright ... Lots of even tracks and an occasional up and down. Two longer breaks and some clouds to beat away some of the heat. At mile 326 we wondered why nobody would enjoy their pizza at this popular spot ...

There was another picknick area, two more miles down. Eventually, those 18 miles turned into 20. With our last ounce of energy we were cheered and applauded at by 15-20 hikers, welcoming us to reach our goal at around 7pm. That was sooo cool!

We had pizza at 9pm and now we are off to sleep ...

Zzzzzz ...

Today, there was some rain followed by an amazing rainbow. The air was super most and windy and we only had a short break whilst hiking toward Interstate 15 at the Cajon Pass. We heard a trailangel hiker would drive to the next REI so we'll stay right here at the "Best Western" at the highway in order to check out REI and get new shoes for Finn tomorrow.

We ended the evening with around 10 hikers in a tiny hot tub ... there were "Feathers", "Bandit", "Sir Loin", "Tylor", Snack Pack", "McGyver" and a few more. "Bounce-Box" arrived and the hotel even offers to send it.

We had an utterly delicious breakfast at the hotel and trailangel Briana drove us to the next REI for 25$ gas money. Both of us acquired new shoes and a small Nalgene for cold nights. We left our old "Trail Runners" Brooks Caldera 2 at Cajon Pass. Let's hope breaking in the new shoes won't take long.

Today we only managed to hike 5 miles because we only left at 5pm. When we reached the camping spot, "Sunshine", Zack, "Bandit", Alexa & Alice, Lulu and Parker were already there. Despite a distance of 5 miles to the highway, you'd still hear traffic and the trains as well.

Tomorrow it'll be upward only, without any sources of water ...

A classic Nero. Not a Zero, not a hero but a Nero. Nearly a Zero or nearly a hero, something in between. Sounds confusing but it's actually simple.

Spending half the day enjoying the amenities of civilization and yet doing some miles. Clearing your conscience by advancing a little further toward Canada.

Usually, these days start by planning a minor breakfast in town before getting back on track. A minor breakfast turns into a brunch and running into fellow hikers makes a common lunch inevitable. Eventually, we do get back on track before doing at least a few more miles.

Sometimes, however, it happens that the indulged energy from a burger and three liters of coke push you into ascending the 8 mile climb in a heartbeat. And before you realize it, suddenly you're mounting your tent in darkness on top of the mountain feeling as proud as punch. Dinner is usually skipped on days like these as you almost fall asleep whilst blowing up your air mattress.

Sunrise and moonset, as well as sunset and moonrise – The days' highlights

I'll attempt to describe the fascination, the pure magic we feel every time the sun sets, knowing she'll be back the next day. More beautiful and wonderful than the day before.

During our journeys, you had always been enthralled by this sun-moon-magic. Whenever the moon doesn't only show up in darkness but also, when the sun still spell casts smiles on our faces with its embracing sun rays – that's when you ask me, whether you could also witness this right now on the other side of the planet – back at home.

We can't always see them and yet we are always ensured: They're there!

The alarm clock rings – snooze.
It rings again – snooze.
And my phone wakes us up once more.
"Finni?"
"Hmm ..."
"We have to get up!"
"Just two more minutes alright?!"
You hug me.
The alarm clock rings again. We get up.

The head lamps supply just the light we need to pack our stuff, while the sky in the East turns into a soft purple already.

Our backs toward the constellations in the night while focusing on the brightening horizon, as we quickly dismantle our transportable home into our backpacks. Backpacks back on, energy bars ready to fuel us and off we go. With the lamps on our heads, chewing on the bars and the hiking sticks in our hands you try to convince your feet of handling another day so they better get used to it.

It's 6:30am and the sun slowly emerges behind the mountains. With every breath I take to advance toward the sun, the cold morning air tickles my nose, and when breathing out, small clouds float out of my mouth. It's cold.

But then single, gentle rays of sun slowly warm up your skin. We halt, stay in silence, close our eyes and fully live in the moment. We let the energy warm and refuel us, for what is ahead of us.

We are like paralyzed. Neither wanting to advance nor wanting to go back. Warming up our bodies from the cold night but we're fully aware it's about to be hot in a few hours – really hot.

We're sweating and our sweat cools us down a little. Are longing for clouds to provide us the required shade. Drinking as much as we can to replenish the fluids gone with the sweat.

And then there is the moment you stop caring. No matter how much you're sweating, no matter how hot it is, how bad you're smelling, you just keep going. You're on the move like everyone else, are sweating like everyone else and stinking like everyone else. You've reached a point at which your own smell wakes you up in the night whenever you raise your arm above your head. Doesn't matter, you conclude, you'll have a shower in four days.

During noon it's tough, the heat gets to your head.

You can't think straight and sometimes you see the stars although it's not night time yet. You're sucking once more on the tube that's connected to the most precious item you're carrying: The water container.

You keep sipping all the way until it's finally: "Dammit, I think I'm out of water."

"It's all good, I think I have some left. Have some."

You're carefully sipping, wetting your lips. Taking a tiny sip and trying to divide it into even tinier portions to swallow. Economizing where you shouldn't have to economize.

"Don't worry, take some more, I don't need it.", I'm telling you, but you're responding ever so sweetly, "It's all good, I just need a sip, you need it more. Have to watch out with your kidney. Drink up!"

Shortly later on we finally reach a spring. Chugging one liter immediately.

As the sun reaches its zenith, we're having a siesta. Down here in the desert it's still okay to rest until temperature have cooled down. Once we'd reach Northern California, it won't be that easy, as we'll be focused on doing more miles a day.

That's how you keep evaluating day by day, weighing off miles for water sources, heat and camping spots.

Once you'd arrive at a suitable location to spend the night, you'd prepare the meal you had been longing for all the way and watch the sun slowly setting toward the horizon.

"Look, the moon has already come up. What time is it in Germany?"

"Nine hours later. So it'd be night over there", I'm responding.

"Just imagine how it's the very same moon that Meike and Birger were to watch if they looked outside right now. Crazy, right? So far and yet we're seeing the same!"

Another moment, where you remind me of the fact that regardless of where we are, we're always having a connection to back home.

I begin to smirk and look at you completely in love.

Now the sky turns colorful. Reaching from orange over red all the way to a blazing red. We're just sitting there staring into the sun and enjoying the moment. We're in silence and thankful for this moment.

You can't really grasp what exactly is so captivating about this view but it doesn't matter anyway. Every single evening we were so happy to watch this ever so beautiful sunset out in nature day by day.

You're sitting as you're reminiscing about the day, recalling beautiful moments and are looking forward to the next day despite all the pain.

"AS", you're shouting and rip me out of my thoughts. That's our warning call when we're approaching an ant trail that we jump across.

I quickly lower my head and watch all these hundreds of tiny black dots swarm toward one direction. What appears to be utter chaos to us humans is in fact unbelievably organized. Nature – completely fascinating!

This miracle of nature that manages to replace animal documentaries – and that is happy about some leftover pasta that fell off our plates.

I'm chuckling in thoughts while stirring through my now mashed pasta and leaning toward the breathtaking sunset.

There she goes, descending behind the trees and yet one enjoys this happening. One doesn't mourn this, however, because you know: She is not gone, you just can't see her anymore. And there is the moon already. Radiating in total clarity and accompanied by millions of stars to illuminate your tent, making you wish to sleep with eyes open. You're staring into the sky, stunned by this view, counting the shooting stars and slowly fall asleep.

DAY 33   05/01/2019   MILE 347 - 364

Today we only marched uphill for 15 miles straight, wearing our new shoes. I ended up with two blisters at the heels of which just now I beautifully tore one off with the tape. Finn also has his heels taped and a fully blown blisters squeezes out from the side. It feels odd to now walk around in boots as they're much heavier and obviously have to be broken in first. We were, however, rewarded with beautiful views today, one of which was a rainbow-sky.

Today, it's sleeping at 8.200ft, sleeping bags attached together and baby Nalgene is filled with hot water.

DAY 34   05/02/2019   MILE 364 - 369

Been sleeping in nicely and being the last to leave the camping spot toward Wrightwood. My day wasn't great and so we decided to hop in to Wrightwood since we'd need some food for the coming 6-7 days. Hitchhiked to town and went straight to the brewery. After two beers we decided to go to "budpharm.com" together with "Dumbo" and "Sir Parsley". The owner Dave picked us up and we had delicious dinner at the "farm", followed by Nutella Crêpes for dessert. They also had chickens and donkeys at the weed farm.

We all know the elephant with the big ears known as Dumbo. But this one doesn't come with big ears, but with a cloth beneath his cap that the wind blows and giving him Dumbo-like ears.

Other than this, he has no similarities with the cute little elephant. "Dumbo" comes with brown, long dreads he takes good care of. A black beard, also well taken care of, especially when considering he has access to electricity, clean water and a shower only every 5-10 days.

He is a calm person with a soft temper. Every time you'd come across him having lunch, he'd be reading a book while waiting for his instant-noodles to be soaked. He is never in a hurry and is always easy going. Always up for a good conversation as he crochets his dread locks. We keep running into him, keep passing each other and march together through snow and ice up in the Sierra.

DAY 35   05/03/2019   MILE 369 - 384

We managed to fall back asleep after being woken up by a super loud rooster, before hearing him "announce" the day for a second time. A quick shower while trying to touch as little as possible, for it wasn't exactly clean at the "farm". We kept our breakfast short and went back on track.
5 miles till the bottom of Mt. Baden Powell before a steep ascent of 4 miles. It was so much snow for the last 1.5 miles that it really was just straight up without winding tracks. Up at the peak we enjoyed the magnificent view that rewarded us for all the pain once again. The book showed us that Tyler and Jaja "Snack Pack" had been up here ahead of us. Two days before also "Hot Foot" and "Skippy Skunk".
Another 6 miles down and shortly before darkness fell, we reached "little Jimmi" Camp. The food is safely stored inside the bear boxes. (With "Joy Ride" at the Bade Powell).

DAY 36   05/04/2019   MILE 384 - 399,5 (400)   *TRAILMAGIC*

Today it was lots of ups and downs, very steep ascents and descent ... Hence, trail magic at Buckhorn Campground was exactly what we needed. Burgers were made (even veggie ones) and there were plenty of cold beverages (also beer ♥♥), candy, bananas and oranges. As unexpected as it always is, the happiness of trail magic is always massive!!!

The Buckhorn Campground isn't exactly part of the PCT, but we're having to include this minor detour in order to protect the frogs that appear to be crossing that part of the PCT.

"Next year we'll do the same. Take some weeks off and spend them here at the PCT to provide and supply trail magic. I'll load my backpack with lots of food for the hikers and wander into the Sierra. No one will expect trail magic over there. It'll be rad!", you're saying ever so enthusiastic and I'm responding no less thrilled: "Heck yeah, slick idea. And we can gather with "Sunshine", Ben, Parker and all the others and all we do for three weeks is trail magic. Great, I'm so excited already!"

Being able to return what we now are being given along the way and knowing exactly what the hikers need. To bring unsolicited pleasure and delivering pushes of motivation to every single hiker.

Your idea to create trail magic together with your "traimily" (trail-family) and be back where we had all met a year ago, had helped each other out and had conquered mountains together, is stunningly beautiful. It's talking about the PCT 24/7 and you never get tired of it. To know, that even though one day the path ends, it will go on. It will go on with all the new friends we made that'll enrich us for the rest of our lives.

Today, we took off already at 7:20am and reached Camp Glenwood a mile into the hike. Over there, we had coffee, bathrooms and a banana ♥♥♥. That was where we sent our first post card to Germany from. The owner's (Chuck) son (Wulfi) runs a hostel at Lake Tahoe – we are invited to check it out!

We had some sick tacos (self-made with leftover pasta of the evening before) and saw some deer. Trail magic at the fire station and we were able to plug in the Sawyer at the water tab and thus were able to filter our bottles within 10 minutes. Eating time now.

It was drizzling this morning. Which made it hard to leave the tent. With our rain coats ready we left at 8:15am. The entire day was rather cloudy so we kept our breaks short. No more rain though! A hummingbird gave me company as I was peeing right next to the trail, fortunately nobody passed us as I was sitting with my pants down.
Tomorrow we'll likely head to Agua Dulce.

Another foggy morning to get up into, but today the sun came through rather quickly. We advanced fast across "smaller" hills (also, we had already left at 7:15am) and had ice cream and a Pepsi down at KOA near Acton. Shortly before reaching Agua Dulce, we went through Vasquez Rocks County Park which was pretty cool as we saw some owls. Once we reached Agua Dulce, we shopped for fruits and vegetables and went for "hiker heaven" (trail angel) where we'd shower and eat. Laundry was done at the drop of a hat while I was on the phone with mom. It was here that we met again with Tyler, "Bandit", "Feathers", Vanessa "Little Bee" and many others.

This morning, Finn was driven to a doctor in Santa Clarita by "Ironlady". The doctor removed a piece of his toe nail and checked out the swollen area beneath. Antibiotics and IBU 800 for a couple of days and another zero-day tomorrow. In the afternoon, we went to REI and got new pairs of Trailrunner-shoes and (warmer) sleeping bags. Some expensive fun right there! And Ben "Sir Loin" has arrived.

DAY 41   05/09/2019   ZERO-DAY   AGUA DULCE

Today, we mailed some packages: Sleeping bags to San Diego, boots and crampons to KM and a birthday card and Clif Bar to Steve (unfortunately, it's not allowed to send "fireball"). Sadly, I also learned that Carsten's tumor grew once more and he'll only have a few more days left. I'll be carrying him with me in my thoughts along the way and hope he won't be in pain!!!
We had pizza with Ben and had a fun evening together with Cloe. I'll finish this hike also for Carsten!

"Hiker heaven" was the place to relax and recharge on all levels. Those people provide you with a home equipped with showers, toilets, computers, postal service, washing machines, a kitchen and a living room. You're surrounded by people feeling and thinking exactly the same as you, and once more it's no other topics to talk about but the PCT.

Your big toe has been troubling you since the very start of the journey. It kept inflaming due to the ingrowing toe nail. Often times, sticks and stones would block your foot and you could've peed your pants for the pain you endured. You never complained or whined about it. Pulled yourself together and marched on.
Eventually, when it had gotten unbearable, you saw a doctor.

He suggested to remove the toe nail completely and let it regrow in a clean way.

But once you told him about our business down here, how it would be impossible to keep your toe clean every day, he only cut out a part of it.

It was okay for a while before it inflamed again. Sometimes you just wished to amputate the toe.

Learning to ignore and endure physical pain – you mastered this skill way better than I!

Once we reached "Hiker Heaven", I got emotional pain.

Those news we neither wish to receive, nor to be true, always hit unexpectedly and you feel like their sole purpose is to hit the receiver really hard. As was I.

The news on Carsten struck me like a fist!

I sent pictures to him, wanting to show him where I was all because of him and how beautiful it was down here. I knew, he was already stuck to his bed and couldn't really do anything at all.

Wanted to cheer him up and display how I was trying to turn his completely fucked up situation a little better.

By going on a hike – taking him with me.

My message to him:
"Hello hello from the peak of Baden Powell.
We left the peak, however, already about a week ago behind us ... now we're in Agua Dulce and mastered some 730km already. Three weeks from now we'll go from desert up the High Sierra into the mountains, facing snow every day for 6 weeks

on an altitude between 3.000m and 4.000m.
We've both gotten quite fit, though.
Best wishes (still) from Southern California"

The response is simply:
"My life is ending. All the best. It was beautiful!"

I'm completely done, start crying and fall into your arms. You catch me, as you always do whenever I'm down. Then I'm making a phone call to my friend Laura and she suggest me to tell him once more that it was because of him that I made the decision to walk this trail.

Hence, I did and I'm writing to him, how thankful I was to have gotten to know him, thankful for everything he taught me and that his destiny made us take on this journey.

One month later his wife delivers the message that he fell asleep in her arms with a smile on his face.

I'm receiving the news in Mammoth, a location deep in the Sierra. Crying and not knowing, how I'll possible be able to get back on track. Always wondering about the same question: Why?

But nobody answers this question for you. And even if, that wouldn't bring him back.

I'm angry, for it is so unfair. I'm sad, for I'll never see him again. I'm worried about his family.

Then it's back to the trail ... and suddenly, there's a turning point. I'm becoming grateful for the time we shared, happy to have gotten to know him and I'm sensing the fighting spirit in my head to never ever give up on this trail. To eliminate the words "give up" from my vocabulary and to fight. Charging every tough situation in my life with the sole purpose of winning and to keep going no matter what. Because Carsten did so.

From now on, he is with us. He is with us with every foot step. Enjoys the views and the freedom of nature – just like us.

DAY 42 05/10/2019 MILE 454 - 465

Today, we were taken downtown by the truck at around 12pm and had pizza once more with Ben, before taking off. We managed to demount the tent while it was still drying but we quickly reached some drizzling, foggy clouds. After about 11 miles we mounted the tent and are lying in our new sleeping bags.

Just when we were about to leave Agua Dulce, we saw the Dutchmen "The Flying Dutchman" and his daughter arrive. ...We had been sure, they were long ahead of us ... that's how you always meet each other again!

DAY 43 05/11/2019 MILE 465 - 478

We left super late because it was raining tonight and we waited until the sun dried up the tent. The weather was really sticky because of all the rain so the hike was hard on me. After merely 6 miles we napped at a beautiful location beneath some trees (cave) and then quickly marched to "Casa de Luna".

We were welcomed by about 30-40 hikers and there was delicious taco-salad. The Anderson's (Jo & Terri) are super kind and will even make pancakes for everyone tomorrow.

You're making a plan. There was supposed to be a massive party on our return. We wanted to have all of our friends coming and tell them all about our experiences. Lots of beer, preferably entire barrels and delicious food – taco salad – was supposed to be served.

"How delicious was that?!! We'll have to do this for sure when we're back – for our party! You can easily do a vegetarian or vegan version of this. It's perfect for everyone!"

"Most definitely, let's do this. Rad idea!", I'm responding no less excited.

DAY 44   05/12/2019   MILE 478 - 493

This morning we had the best pancakes ever! Made by Jo! We were given a yoga session by "Snakesharmer" in the rising sun and took a good-bye picture with Casa de Luna, the rising moon ;-)

At around 10pm back on the trail, two hours later the first rattle snake. We were minding our business with a snack in the shade and it curled up from behind, passed our backpacks by 3ft and eventually found itself inside a tree across the path.

We had another 2 small, well camouflaged rattle snakes and a huge swarm of bees flying directly toward us before turning and moving up the mountain.

Additionally, those black, cockchafer-like beetles are everywhere, moving their butt up when jumping over them. Today it was pretty hot but only a third of the 15 miles was an ascent, the rest was easy-peasy. Finn's trail names:

"Huckleberry", "Jaws", "Sir Burps-A-Lot", "Colorful", "Jack Black" (JB) ...But he can't decide between them all ...

That trail name thing is totally new to us and for the Americans a big deal. It's a pseudonym, a chance to being someone else out here. You'd notice from the very start that the Americans were all eager to receive their trail name. Exactly, to receive it. Because you're given a trail name, it's not like you're choosing it. It either reflects your spirit, your optics or tells a memorable story.

We were never really after being awarded a trail name, which is why you had gathered those suggestions for a while.

But you wouldn't just go for one.

Fourty-four days later, your voice busts through the monotonous grating sound of the sandy trail.

"You know what, Larry?"

"Tell me"

"I've got the perfect trail name for me!"

"Oh really, and which one would that be?", I'm asking with the eyebrows upwards.

"Puffin!"

"Hmm? What is Puffin? What does that even mean?"

"Puffin is the English term for those birds that are famous in Iceland."

"And how come this would be your perfect trail name?", am I wondering, not really being convinced so far.

"It's very simple. For one thing, they sport a colorful beak just like my cap and board shorts. They enjoy going for a dive and have fish – just like me. And the name "fin" is part of theirs. I prefer the name "Finn" with one "n" anyway."

Full of excitement now myself, am I having to slow down all your enthusiasm and point out the fact that it's not part of the game to choose a trail name yourself.

But your solution is just around the corner: "Well, then you'll just randomly have to drop the idea once we are gathering with Ben, Tyler and the others."

Sigh. "This name just seems too perfect.", am I responding. "They don't even know you love fish and eagerly go for a dive. But I'll give it a shot". I'm smiling completely in love and keep on walking.

Shortly afterwards, people increasingly point out your colorful and vivid clothing, calling you the most flamboyant guy on the trail. That's where I took the lead and simply put down "Larissa and Colors" into the next trail register.

Henceforth, you are not introducing yourself as Finni but as "Colors". It's a done deal.

DAY 45   05/13/2019   MILE 493 - 508

Today, we started fairly early (8am). But we went to get water after half a mile, which meant an additional hour as the source was a mile away off track and out of a sudden it was 9:30am. We walked a lot in the shade and encountered some trail magic.

In the burning heat, uphill and without any supportive shade, we chalked off the milestone for mile number 500. Once we did that, we had a shot of "fireball" with "Easy Strider", "Wyld Card" and "Chipmunk".

Then we spotted a water tank with bear's corpse. So we didn't get water but waited for the next spring.

The bag of water, bottles and the Saywer (water filter) in the left hand and the walking stick in the right hand. That's how I get going. The path is easy, just following the dirt track. It gets steeper and I start running when suddenly I trip and start to slide. "Slow down", I'm thinking. "Finni will get mad if I know fall and bust my ankle".

I do slow down, climb over branches, jump puddles and can already make up the creek down the slope between the two hills.

"So I'll have to return back up all that – except fully loaded with water", are my sudden thoughts. "Hopefully Finn will have food prepared by then, I'm starving."

Then it hits me that he can't prepare food without the water I'm about to bring back up. I'm starting to move faster again.

Once at the creek, it's the same procedure as every time.

Opening the water bag, shoving it against the stream, filling it up and closing it. Carefully inclining the water bottles to have them flooded, waiting, full. Then mounting the Sawyer onto the water bag and checking it's tight. It's always a hassle to perfectly mount the Sawyer without water leaking out the screwing mechanism.

Afterwards, squeezing the empty bottle between the feet, turning the water bag and filter on top with care and pushing.

We never measured the time but it does take a while for the two liters to run through and supplying us with drinkable water in the Nalgene-bottle.

Here I am, crouched down and thinking about all the bear excrements we came across today.

Then it strikes me. Bears, a spring, the sun setting. Perhaps I better hurry and return to the others, before mama bear joins for a drink together with her cups.

Second bottle loaded, lid locked and filling the water bag and the bottle a second time.

"I'll run the filter back up at Finni", are my thoughts.

I'm starting to feel uneasy. Keep looking around and start to talk to myself in a loud voice, I randomly sing a song and eventually laugh at myself.

It feels like eternity to me, and not only to me as I later learn to know, before being back up with the five liters of water. The walking stick back into the right hand am I hustling uphill and grab the bottles with my whole strength. The water bag tingles down from the left hand.

The way seems like forever – and there it is, a loud cracking noise that is not mine. I halt, turn around and squeeze my eyes to increase my vision – no bear in sight.

"Please don't be a mountain lion", am I hoping.

My breath slows down, my heart beat increases and I start sweating all around. Then I see him.

It was another hike coming down – what a massive relief!

"Hi, still far away? Oh and by the way, your boyfriend already got worried about you."

"Oh, ok, thanks! Yeah, no, it's just around the corner there", is my response and I march on.

Once I'm back on top, you stare at me with big eyes.

"Where were you? I thought something happened to you. I was about to come looking for you"

"No, man, that was a super long way and I already filtered back down. Is the food ready?", am I wondering, ever so hopeful.

"Yes, thankfully I had some water left in my Platypus."

I was the happiest person on Earth.

Water is the most important element on the trail. Without water, we humans can't survive. As opposed to other hikers that sometimes start their journey with 10 liters of water, we always have to look out for water during the trail. Springs, rivers, lakes, snow, ice and sometimes a "water cache".

A spring is the best option by far. The ability to directly drink from it without having to filter it, purely beautiful. We started doing that only a while later, though. At some point, you simply stop caring really; just put your bottle beneath the fresh spring water and drink it as it is. The most natural and beautiful way to satisfy your thirst!

Often times, we come across rivers, creeks and springs without having to do major detours off the PCT. Our map displays most of the water sources and it allows you well to calculate how much you'll need for the next part. Before we get going, chugging down another liter. Anything you're not having to drag along is a gift.

Sometimes, however, you do have to do a detour to be getting that water. If possible, you'll leave your backpack by the trail, hoping no rodents will creep up your food. You walk these extra feet, sometimes miles, just to provide enough water for the coming stretch.

The stretches in the desert can easily be divided according to the springs. You walk from one spring to the next one and try to camp as close as possible to a spring, avoiding to carry more water. One tries to avoid "dry camping". Which means not carrying water for dinner, for the night, brushing teeth all the way to the next water source.

Got off early once more (7:30am) and faced only 10 miles before reaching hiker town. Over there, we checked out a café/restaurant/shop (Wee Vill Market) and had a break until 5pm. Refilled our water to the max as the next stretch would be through plain desert for 18 miles without any springs. That's why we plan on walking this at night. We met "Easy Strider" and "Pringles" again around 5:45pm and got going with some 8 guys toward Los Angelas Aguadulce. After a while we saw that group of "Sunshine", Parker and the sisters but parted ways due to a major break.

We advanced quickly also because "Easy Strider" and "Wyld Card" are pretty tall. "Easy Strider" almost stepped on a snake. Apart from that and some coyotes in the distance the night remained calm. We arrived at the spring at 1:30am and camped with about 25-30 other hikers.

"Easy Strider" and "Wyld Card", also known as "The Twin Towers". Both tall, skinny and doing huge steps while managing to look completely relaxed.

He sports long, blond hair reaching across his chest, a scattered but long beard and a desert-grey cowboy hat. His combination of a beige shirt, a dark grey t-shirt beneath, dark long pants and worn out hiking boots makes him appear even taller. He resembles Gandalf from Middle Earth with his long face and incredibly long arms and legs, out here looking for the Good – but in this story he calls himself "Easy Strider".

I think the first time we really met was in Agua Dulce in "Hiker Heaven". His calm but open mind always let to great conversations. During "night hike", he spoke a lot about the brewery he was keen on opening together with his pal. Perfect topic to talk about for a long, boring stretch. You also loved talking to him for hours.

"Wyld Card" also has many stories to tell. He is constantly talking, usually revolving around his back pain, the fights with his girlfriend and after all, he doesn't really know why he is here in the first place. Quite the funny character who isn't really part of the "ultra-light hikers" considering his equipment. His cousin gave him the backpack and before you showed him how to properly install it, he wouldn't stop trying to adjust it, fiddle with it and moving it around. Seat cushions aid him fitting the belt correctly. You always lose it when seeing how terrible the backpack sits on his back. His way of putting on the backpack, however, amazes you every time and you try to imitate it.

A regular tent adds up to his backpack which fits perfectly into the 70-liter backpack despite its size. His ripped "Long Johns" are covered with board shorts and the worn out sneakers he's been using for really long are still surviving on the PCT. To deal with the back pain, that according to him, in no way whatsoever is related to his amazing pair of shoes and all the weight, we pause every hour for him to intake some THC.

After all, our "night hike" was quite fun and not one bit boring. The regular breaks weren't too bad as I had trouble keeping up with the two giants thanks to my short legsies.

And then there is "Pringles", Martina, whom "Wyld Card" really is into. Also tall, skinny and just by herself – making her hot stuff at the trail. Perhaps that's why she asked to be doing "night hike" together.

She's from Czech Republic and we had met a few days prior during a drinking break. There she was, sipping her healthy-looking shake by the spring, where we had gone to because of the dead bear lying at the other spring.

When I asked about her drink, she said it's a mixture assembled back in Czech Republic just for her.

Later on at Wee Vill Market I made an order as well because I should be doing something against my weight loss. Not really cheap but super healthy – I now have ordered four kilograms of protein powder. That should do the job to refill my energy and fortify my strength to take on the nearing High Sierra and everything else we'll encounter.

DAY 47   05/15/2019   MILE 535 - 549

This morning I got up still tired and feeling groggy. We crossed some hills approaching the mountains. It was somehow hot and windy and we'd just feel exhausted!
Everyone!
Most likely because we all had a lack of sleep due to the night hike, we were hungry and just felt beat.
We finally reached the next spring ahead of noon and had a long break. Got going around 4pm equipped with lots of water on our backs, to move up another 2.000ft. It's rather windy and tonight it's supposed to rain as of 2am onward but it's just another 9.5 miles to Tehachapi.

It had started drizzling during the night and thankfully there was no massive wind, because the sandy ground would have easily loosened the tent pegs. Rain intensified a little once we got going but just for an hour or so. Time flew by as we marched those 9.5 miles to the street which is where we met "Easy Strider" and "Wyld Card" who had just called a "trail angel" to pick them up and drive them to town. So we hitched their ride. When later on meeting "Sir Parsley" and the Canadians "Bearclaw" and "Watermelon" we decided on Branda's Place (another trail angel). So here we are, freshly showered and did groceries already, too. And we had sushi today ♥♥♥.

DAY 49   05/17/2019   "LAS VEGAS"

This morning we got the news that the heavy storm forces some hikers into retreat. They're facing a wind speed of up to 60 mph and strong snow storm.
So people had to adjust their plans this morning and decide how to get back to the trail.
"Pringles" will head to San Francisco for a few days ... The other group with "Sunshine", Parker and the girls weren't able to make up their minds yet, and together with "Bearclaw" Frank and "Watermelon" Meghan decided to go to Las Vegas.
At the supermarket Finn met Lara and Dan who are going to Hawaii.
After a 3.5 hour drive we hit Las Vegas. Crazy city!
All the lights literally flashed us and we first went to grab

a bite. Afterwards, we checked out a casino at "The Strip".
We play roulette and Meghan finished her game making
39$. I, too, had some 70$ gains in between, but finishing the
game becomes hard ... you could be flipping some of that ;-)
We spent the night camping about half an hour away.

"Watermelon" (Meghan) and "Bearclaw" (Francis) are a couple from French Canada with a great sense of humor. They had
been best friends before losing sight of each other just to eventually start a relationship.

Day 7 in Julien both were sitting at a table at a café. She sport-
ed a turquoise shirt, long light brown hair with minor curls,
put up into a braid. Wearing a cap she was yelling into her cellphone. You'd immediately notice her French accent. Her backpack in 90s colors leaned against a bench along with the other
hikers' backpacks. The place was completely packed but she
didn't care at all. Both were calling back home. Had I paid more
attention back in French class I'd have understood every word
right now. You and I looked at each other – rather annoyed – it
had to be them Frenchmen.

We stumbled across them every now and then and found out
they had already been at the trail last year. Francis had broken
his foot in Northern California and Meghan had to carry him
along with his backpack all the way to the next road, before they
moved heaven and earth to start over the whole thing again this
year. And here they are, knowing every stone, every river and
every spot for the first three or four months. Unbelievable, but
starting over where they previously had left was out of the question. It had to be a "Thruhike"! Very impressive! Thus, I with-
drew the quick prejudice I had installed earlier.

They're just continuing to use the trail names they had been issued last year. "Watermelon" simply got the name because she'd constantly chew on wine gum shaped like a watermelon. "Bearclaw" always considered the possible encounter of bears a piece of cake and claimed: "If there's ever a bear, I'll fight!"

We shared great laughs at Branda's in Tehachapi for we all didn't take ourselves too seriously. Francis always had troubles pronouncing English properly. But now he proudly announces his ability to distinguish between "bear", "beard", "beer" and "berry", and his very recent achievement is to differentiate between "hangry", "angry" and "hungry". It's not as convincing, however, as he pronounces "hangry" and "angry" in the exact same way. You and I totally lose it and crack up. I'm terribly failing at trying to explain his unconscious silencing of the "h" in the beginning of a word. He just won't get it.

We're having lots of fun together and a great time.

I'm witnessing many similarities between their and our relationship, both being super easy-going. Perhaps it's because we both had been pretty much best friends ahead of the relationships.

It was never about whether or not we'd go to Vegas – it was about "now" or "immediately".

DAY 50   05/18/2019   "VEGAS"   (AN ENTRY BY FINN)

Breakfast at Subway and off to REI. Got a refund for 320$ and off to the Strip, before slipping into "Planet Hollywood", prior to which we had wraps in the parking lot.
Friends of "Bearclaw" and "Watermelon" had tickets for a comedy show. We went to the casino and did penny slots

and played roulette. "Willy Wonka" turned 45 cents into 70$ in just 20 seconds. We ran out of luck playing roulette. Whilst enjoying a beer by the machine, "Willy" was back and flipped 6$ into 38$. Then it was time to sleep at the cold hotel room. Before we had a burger at Gordon Ramsey.

DAY 51   05/19/2019   "VEGAS"   (AN ENTRY BY FINN)

Huge "Wicked Spoon Buffet" in Vegas (it was off the rail) followed by a quick snack with "Hotpants" and "Medici Man" in the hotel room we went toward the G-C. The lookout points were all closed and it was dark and rainy. The boys of the firefighters helped us reach a motel (Canyons End Motel).
We're hoping to see the canyon tomorrow morning.

DAY 52   05/20/2019   ZERO-DAY   TEHACHAPI

Unfortunately, no Grand Canyon :(We went all the way from the motel to the parking lot at the Grand Canyon Visitor Center just to learn that we won't be able to check out the Grand Canyon without booking a tour (the cheapest one for 60$).
We were late anyway as we had to return the car the latest by 5pm.
Had a small, very brief stop at Hoover Dam and were back in Tehachapi at 5pm. The weather is still shitty but we could go back to Brenda's.

On day 53, we went the 8 miles from the first turn off (after Tehachapi) together with some other folks that were at Brenda's as well to the second turn off ...slack packing... then said goodbye to "Bearlcaw" and "Watermelon".
In the evening, we hung out at Marriot Fairfield Inn Hotel with Ben "Sir Loin" and some other 30 hikers. All together we'd enjoy the hot tub. Lots of beer, booze and pad thai.

On Wednesday, Meike and Birger dropped by at 2pm and we went for delicious food at Village Grill. Then we checked out all our pictures and went re-supplying together. Afterwards, we were off to "Tehachapi" ... very delicious! In the evening it was movie and beer in bed!

Today we had delicious breakfast together with Meike and Birger at the hotel, did laundry and prepared the "bounce box" that we now send to Lake Tahoe, after it had been sent to Helge and Elke by accident.
At the post office we met "Neddy Lite", "Faucet", Richard and Ben. They wanted to rent a car and drive to Ashland to go "SoBo". I don't think there'll be less snow by now!
Meike and Birger drove us to the trail head and said goodbye! 6 miles uphill and the last two through mud! When mounting our tent, it started to rain ... just perfect.

We were so happy to see Meike and Birger – your parents. They came visit Elke and Helge in San Diego and most certainly wanted to see us, too, on this occasion. The plan was to meet in Idyllwild because we loved that place and thought it would give a great insight into the "hiker lifestyle". Due to the weather, the distance and lack of time we changed that plan and had a good time at a hotel room in Tehachapi. With beer in bed and browsing through pictures on TV.

How precious and beautiful for you three to have met one last time! You being able to show them the surroundings we encountered ourselves in and sharing some "hiker trash" with them. Even if it were just a few hours, it was perfect and simply amazing, that they drove up to us.

Meike and Birger, it was the last time you guys got to see your Finni boy. To feel him and hold him in your arms. Caressing his hair one final time, looking him in the eyes and getting to breathe his scent.
One last picture before we turn around, get going and disappear behind the mountain.

At this moment, I'd like to point out to you that writing down these memories was highly motivated by giving you guys the possibility of getting an insight into the beautiful last months that Finn lived.
Letting you two know, how happy he was and how he lived life to the fullest and enjoyed every bit of it.
He loved every minute of the PCT and would always wake up to eagerly dive into the next adventure.

He spread an unbelievable amount of joy for life and shared it with everyone he'd meet out there.

Unfortunately, we won't be able to experience any further adventures with Finn, but he lives on! Also, by telling his adventures.

Take this book and his adventure at the PCT as "Colors" will remain. He'll live on as a son, a brother, an uncle, a partner and a friend.

To the little Birk he will be talked about as that one uncle, that never ceased to dodge an adventure and would always be "ready to go", no matter where to.

Ready to help out anyone and simply adorable. Honest and full of integrity. Who believed in Karma and who wasn't let down by this belief. Talented in (almost) all areas, a jack of all trades to fear no work ever. Intelligent, smart and down for dumb shit. Coming up with new ideas on a daily basis and keen to learn new things every time. He'd give people the shirt off his back to ensure everyone was fine.

You brought an incredible and fascinating human to life and raised him the best way. I am so happy to have gotten to know Finn that one day that you, Birger, drove him to school. You guys were late and he was the last person to enter the class room when immediately catching my attention – paving the road for my new part of life.

But you have two other kids, who are no less amazing. Three beautiful kids – forever, regardless, of whatever will happen.

They are each stunning in their own ways and yet do they share similarities in one way or another.

When Leif snores, I'm hearing Finn. When Jonna has the hick-ups, I hear Finn. When Leif puts on working clothes, I see Finn. When Jonna makes funny faces, I see Finn. And also when I'm around you guys, I sense Finn. Because he is there, because you're all carrying him with you.

Even if we can't have Finn physically in our arms no more, he is in fact with us. We feel him, see him and hear him. Perhaps not the way like before, but if we carefully listen to our spirits, he is there!

DAY 56   05/24/2019   MILE 577 - 596,5

Got going pretty late this morning, 8:30 am, but started with sunshine and had a beautifully sunny day, except for some clouds here and there, which, however, is quite nice during a hike. We saw two skunks and a few squirrels. After 14 miles, our feet were hurting and so was Finn's back due to the heavy backpack. We're really feeling that one week off so we're having to get used to the drill again.

DAY 57   05/25/2019   MILE 596,5 - 612

Again, left only at 8:30am and hiked through some foggy woods for the first two hours where we spotted three cows out of nowhere. Sun came through later on and we had another stunning day, through forest and alongside tiny, enchanting creeks, fueled by last week's rain.

Around afternoon, our feet still hurt like hell! It's probably because of the heavy backpacks but we do need supplies for another five days for which each we carry 4 liters of water as the next spring is still 30 miles away.

We had our first glance of the Sierra when passing the mountain.

DAY 58   05/26/2019   MILE 612 - 631

Broke records in taking off at 6:55 am – brushing our teeth with a view of the mountains. Demounted the tent without the forecast rain and off through the "ice-cold" "Mojave Desert" (during May/June it's usually 100-110°F up there). Now, the daily max is 53°F...but with the proper, thicker clothing that sure is easier to handle than fighting 110°C – without any shade. Saw many Joshua trees but no Mojave-Turtle ;-)

Arrived at the water cache...and there is still some water left. Once the tent was mounted, it started pouring ... perfect timing!

DAY 59   05/27/2019   MILE 631 - 651

Woke up in the morning ... dry tent ... yayyy

Packed quickly and refilled the bottles at the water cache. To our surprise, we met "Pringles". We felt super cold this morning, so the 1.500ft climb was just right to heat up. We had just "defrosted" when we hit snow at the "Mojave Desert". The scenery was simply amazing and when we descended at the other side of the mountain, the melted snow poured onto us. Today was a fairly easy hike. Lots of descent and only in the morning some uphill. Were lucky again with the weather as the sky cleared up toward noon. And we saw a snake (gopher) once more, that seemed to be enjoying the sunrays after such a cold night. After 20.5 miles we arrived at the Walker Pass Campground where trail magic expected us – in the shape of super delicious pasta with veggie sauce.

DAY 60   05/28/2019   MILE 651 - 669

Kicked off the day with freshly brewed coffee and pancakes. Again starting the hike uphill ... really quite steep. Once we made it on top, we had a fully blown pot of pasta. Apart from some minor hail, we were lucky again in terms of weather. In the afternoon, it even got really hot! Saw another gopher and had absolutely stunning views!!! Tonight we made fire, had a spring close by and enjoyed the beautifully soothing sound of crickets – that's how you sleep! Good night.

DAY 61   05/29/2019   MILE 669 - 689   (AN ENTRY BY FINN)

We seem to be having a run! Left straight at 7am and hustled straight up for 10km! Lunch break was a warm meal and then downward to the water. Filtered some 8 liters and then back uphill for another 10km (the last ones in the desert). Half way through we got ravenous but sadly we're out of snacks! We guzzled the glass of peanut butter in order to gain strength – and to avoid our moods turning. After 20 miles, everything is hurting. A quick bite, saving two bees, doing number in the open meadows with a view of the trail and then good night! Tomorrow it'll be 13 miles to Kennedy Meadows! (downhill)

"Hi Finn, I need to relieve myself."

"Sweety ... surely you must be joking?! We just left half an hour ago, why couldn't you just do it back then?", you're asking somewhat annoying but I do see a minor smirk on your face.

"Well, I just couldn't back then ... My body has to warm up first."

Walked the talk. As soon as I put my mouth where my thoughts were, my intestine makes some noise. Staying on track, step by step, am I browsing the landscape for an ideal spot to do my business.

Every single step puts a blow through my whole body, forcing me to tighten up my butt cheeks at all cost. There is a fine line between wanting to run and lowering the pace as to minimize risk. Everything is tight.

"How about here?"

"No, people would see.", am I countering the suggestion.

We keep marching.

"And here?"

"Suck as well. Perhaps over there, around the turning corner."

Slowly I'm becoming nervous. The pressure increases and the closer I get to the target area, the less I feel able to hold in any longer. I halt, scan the way in front and behind me – clear. No other hiker about to join the party and the spot looks feasible.

I drop my hiking sticks into the grass. You'd always complain whenever I did that, claiming they'd deform and I might as well just stick them into the ground. "Yeah, yeah", I'd always respond just to drop them again the next time. I'm quickly opening the backpack's straps, push it off my back and letting the backpack fall onto the floor, grabbing one of the hiking sticks and get going. Utterly hectic am I turning around again as I forgot the "poop kit". I rip the zipper open of the upper compartment and take out the Ziploc bag with the bathroom amenities. A worn down keep-fresh pack with some holes in it. Inside, a small light shovel, a pack of wet wipes, a roll of toilet paper and another Ziploc for the used toilet paper.

Sharing on poop kit the two of us has the advantage of saving space and weight, but comes with the disadvantage of always having to wait for each other. Except if we were to do number two literally side by side, just like "Watermelon" and "Bearclaw" who dig their cat holes next two each other, squatting knee-by-knee.

I'm starting to run, fully equipped with everything I need. My intestine throws the signal that it's ready to launch. I'm just thinking "but I'm not!"

I leave the trail, upward a small hill and toward high grass, as I watch the perfect spot a few meters ahead. No grass, soft soil and unable to see Finn. It all seems a little too perfect. "Hi Finn", am I yelling at your direction. "Where does this path lead to? Check out the map real quick, I might have found another route."

You burst into laughter.

"I think the PCT continues right there. It follows a curve and continues up where you are. But there's a good spot down here!"

I'm closing my eyes, take a deep breath and tighten my cheeks even a little more and leg it. Ziploc in my left, hiking stick in my right hustling back down to you. You're flashing a massive smirk, recording me with your cell phone, fully amused to watch me struggling to reach the bushes.

Digging the hole real quick, pants down and relieving myself.

"That was damn close, but it is indeed a neat spot. Don't you have to yourself? It's really cool!", I'm shouting to you, fully in ease.

You decide to check out at cashier 5 as well.

The daily evening struggle

I'm opening the small compartment of my backpack's strap. Getting out my cellphone and open up "Guthooks", the navigation app. I've stopped caring about the course of the trail really. Instead, I'm just curious about the difference in altitude and how many miles it'll be uphill, how steep it is and how many miles we'll be going downward. I'm watching the app every 15, then 10 and eventually every 5 minutes. My feet hurt and I'm unable to fully straighten my knees. I'm walking with my back bent, my face distorted in agony and keep thinking "I'm so done". The stomach rumbles which ceases to be even noticed in a sea loaded in pain and tiredness. I'm slowing down and trying to adjust my walking style. Getting the feeling that my legs are stiffening up to ultimately render me unable to walk at all. My hip bones hurt and I shift my backpack every minute. Tighten the straps, move the weight. Loosen them up to relieve my back.

All these miles and yet not really, what we had planned for in the first place. Thirty-three kilometer every day – that had been our initial target distance to master the trail. And now, two months into the hike, it's just a measly handful of miles we've marched so far.

To do more miles in the Sierra? Impossible! So as of Northern California it's gonna be pushing miles, miles and more miles!

I halt, bent down and seek support on my thighs.

"I can't go any further, Finn."

"Oh precious, just a little further. I think, it'll be just around that corner! You can do it! I'm so proud of you!"

"I think I'll have to blast some Harry Potter tunes", I'm telling you with big eyes.

I know you don't like me listening to music. Whenever you want to talk to me or show me something, you'd have to repeat it for I didn't get it the first time. But to take on the final, terrorizing miles, it'd work out best if I were to dive into the beautifully enchanting world of Harry Potter.

You'd always know that. It wasn't for nothing that you kept watching the movies with me whenever I'd feel down. Not because you just loved them – but simply because you knew how to cheer me up.

Hence, now you're just smirking, looking me in the eyes in love and say: "Well then have a ride to Hogwarts and shout-out to Harry."

"Whoa crazy, they're even in the train this very moment on their way to Hogwarts ... how did you know?", I'm laughing and able to suppress my pain for the moment. You wink at me and our hike continues.

I listen carefully and let my thoughts delve into the world of the little wizard, whilst trying to lure my attention into that world and ignoring the pain.

It's a battle between strain and willpower, between giving up and keeping going, crying and laughing and the decision to move step by step.

You're so far ahead of me. Not just in terms of miles, but also in willpower, courage and the strength, to withstand the pain. You're my icon on so many levels.

"Hi Larissa, down here. Look at the tents. We're almost there!", you're eagerly shouting. I'm not fully realizing it and try to squeeze a smile onto my face.

A few minutes later I reach the open, wide meadow. Only now am I noticing the absolutely breathtaking beauty of the view across the open wide with the sun setting in the back. How high up we suddenly are and how cold it has gotten.

We quickly mount our tents. Lying down inside and I start crying. Bursting in tears am I feeling unimaginable pain in my arms and legs. You hold me in your arms, caress me and ensure me, how proud you are of me.

DAY 62 - 64   05/30 - 06/01/2019   MILE 689 - 702 (+ ZERO DAYS)

We mastered the last miles of the desert. After a break down at the water, we walked along the river through beautiful valley landscapes and arrived at Kennedy Meadows (Grumpy Bear) around noon. Over there, we were welcomed with open arms by "Watermelon" (Meghan) and "Bearclaw" (Frank) which was beautiful. A quick beer and Margarita, fixing up two dreadlocks and off the two went toward the Sierra.

Also Tyler, Jaja and "Sunshine" dropped in out of a sudden

in a Jeep. Tyler and Jaja do have to complete that one part of Walker Pass still.

The next day (31 May) we sought/bought our snow equipment ... snow gaiters, an ice axe and bear canisters. Unfortunately, the package containing food that Elke had sent to us had not arrived yet, making us do another zero-day. In the evening we had a "small" party ... We also saw "Oatis" & "Chocolate The White" again ... who are about to go surfing for a week.

This morning (1 June) we packed our stuff after not having gotten too much sleep (because of the "small" party) we received the great news that our package had arrived ... We believe the package with nuts, some bars, a few "Mountain Food", some Ramen was the "better" package of the two.

After squeezing the entire food for 9-10 days into the bear canisters, we went to Kennedy Meadows Grocery Store, where there is going to be movie night under the stars. ... Tomorrow it's off to the Sierra with "Feathers", "Dumbo" & "Horse", Finn and I.

Time had come for me to receive a trail name, too. I should mention that I had gotten some suggestions so far: "Orange", because often times I'd leave a place loaded with oranges in order to stock up some vitamins at least – or "Turtle", because apparently my green rain cover together with my short legsies make me look like a Ninja Turtle from behind. But these suggestions – or "Fanta" as a derivation of "Orange" – all weren't really appealing to me. Thus, I found myself walking to the bottom of the High Sierra without a trail name. And here I am, sitting at a table with a few hikers, stashing my food in the Ziploc-bag.

Suddenly, there is this scrawny wanderer getting up in front of me. His hand carries several used up, utterly dirty keep-fresh bags. He is about to throw them into the garbage and murmurs "No one wants to use these ones, right?!" I'm looking over with my eyes getting bigger. "Oh no, don't throw them. I need those, especially the small ones!" He seems surprised and tells me they have been used and are quite dirty already. "No worries, as long as they weren't your poop kit", I'm smirking and reach happily for the bags. "Feathers" sits next to me and cracks up. "I think I have to give you the trail name "Ziploc" or maybe "Dirty Ziploc". "Yeah, that fits perfectly! She always keeps all our Ziplocs and I'm never allowed to buy new ones", you're shouting at the table.

And thus, so be it. I had no real chance of fighting it anyway, considering all the witnesses at the table. Henceforth, I put down the following names into the trail registers: "Colors" & Dirty Ziploc"

Southern California

The first chapter is done. In two months, we put 700 miles behind us. We started off completely out of shape and are now about to face one of the biggest challenges in our lives.

The High Sierra Nevada.

Majestically, the mountains stand before us and emerge from the valley, covered in sparkling white snow.

I look back at our first part. The desert, that wasn't flat at all and wetter than in previous years. Look back at our first encounters with wild animals and our daily struggle of reaching and surpassing our limits.

We made our first experiences with heat, storm, hail, rain, the cold and snow – grew with it on a daily basis.

Every day prepared us for the next one.

We met so many amazing people. Learned to understand the trail and got to love it more day by day. We taught ourselves to handle pain, hunger and thirst without breaking down. And yet, we have no idea of what's about to come at us.

They say whoever finishes the first 4-6 weeks will finish the whole trail. This, however, doesn't take this year's "High-Snow-Year" into the calculation, where snow won't melt till mid-July, succeeded by fully loaded rivers, making them insanely dangerous. This year, many hikers "flipped", "skipped" or took vacation by the beach for a while. Not us!

The snow is still fresh, the rivers "flat" and Finn a pioneer.

And so it is clear to us – we are going in. Some groups left toward the high mountains a few days before, but it weren't too many. The "bubble" has yet to follow, it's stuck a few weeks behind us.

The snowstorm we had dodged in Vegas was just a week ago and brought massive amounts of snow to the Sierra.

"Let's just see how far we get, we'll still be able to cancel at any time! But without trying I really won't skip this part of the trail!", you're telling anyone that attempts to convince us to skip it.

People wonder whether we've spent nights in snow and ice,

while being fully soaked, whether we do have experience with the ice axe and crampons and whether we do have marched through rivers fully loaded.

"No, but that's the very reason I'm wanting to do it. I want to try it out and make my own experiences!"

Since you have been fully convinced all the way, you have always let me feel utterly safe by your side. You've always given me the feeling to take care of me and to pull through together, no matter what was going to come at us!

Hence, I went with you, totally thrilled and with big expectations of what was next.

From Desert to High Mountains

Welcome to High Sierra Nevada

"We are now in the mountains and they are in us,

kindling enthusiasm, making every nerve quiver,

filling every pore and cell of us."

- John Muir, My First Summer in the Sierra -

Snow – Mountains – Ice – Cold – Lakes – Rivers – Freedom!

Walking, again and again putting one foot in front of the other. The snow crunches below your shoes. Each step leaves a footprint, sometimes more, sometimes less visible.

As soon as the sun rises across the mountains, it becomes difficult. The snow melts and leaves you facing a wet-cold snow desert.

The tiny icy crystals are reflecting the sun, so beautiful and bright. You blink, squint your eyes and it turns black. Quickly putting back on the sunglasses.

You keep sinking ankle-deep into the snow. Pull your foot up, take a deep breath, put down your foot and now you sink up to your calf. Your gaiters support only up to your knee – which is when you feel the icy cold, burning into your nicely warmed up skin.

You're completely exhausted and let go off your hiking sticks, support yourself on the snow with your hands. While trying to get up from the hole, your other leg sinks deeper. As you lay on your side, you take off your backpack in order to put off some weight and pull yourself out.

"The desert section is like your stoner friend,

you get along, you enjoy being around each other,

but he is totally unreliable and not to be trusted."

"The Sierra is the hot girl at the bar...

She's pretty to look at, but is high maintenance,

difficult to be around, and will destroy you emotionally."

Quote from 'Ashes' (Richard Ward)

"Ashes", owner of the quote, is tall, scrawny and looks a bit lost. He wears a makeshift hat made from a brown-green cloth that is supported by small wooden sticks. Green long sleeves and a way too big "Long John". He is the personification of a free spirit. He has a residence just on paper and the plans for upcoming journeys in the mind. He hates the snow and enjoys walking naked.

Unfortunately, our ways parted in South Lake Tahoe as his journey continued elsewhere and he had enough of the PCT.

During our last curry, he shared some great tips with us, also concerning the van we wanted to convert into a camper.

DAY 65   06/02/2019   MILE 702 - 713

We kicked off the day with a fine all-you-can-eat pancake breakfast. Finn tried to refund his socks at TCO ... but they wouldn't have his size left. "Feathers" once again confirmed my trail name "Dirty Ziploc" and Finn introduced himself as "Colors", too.

We shared the bed of a truck with 10 fellow hikers and were taken back to the trail head.

The first ten miles were tough due to the heavily loaded backpacks. About 300ft ahead of reaching the camp, we spotted huge claw marks in a tree from a bear – pretty much on eye level. Had dinner altogether and stored the food that didn't fit the bear canisters inside a tree, before hitting bed fairly early.

DAY 66   06/03/2019   MILE 713 - 728

Left the camp around 6:50am and reached a clearing, partially covered in fog and giving us a stunning view at our next mountains to climb.

After a while, the ascent got steeper and we mounted a small cover when rain kicked in. From 10.000ft onward we ascended through snow and were happy to wear our new gaiters. Descending the mountain was more of slide rather than a walk. The others were expecting us at the camp already when we arrived at 5pm. We made a beautiful fire and dried our shoes. To round off the day, we climbed some rocks as to witness the sunset. *Absolutely amazing!*

DAY 67   06/04/2019   MILE 728 - 743

Again, had stunning landscapes that are just impossible to even remotely capture properly in pictures! During our 4-mile ascent, loud fighter jets would frequent above our heads at perhaps only 300-600ft of altitude. We could feel their bang in our stomachs even with our ears covered. 6.5 miles down to the camp with and without snow left us really exhausted! Some headache due to the altitude but the frog croaking sounds from the pond made up for it.

There is that constant thought, when will "it" come and how can I deal with it?

And suddenly it's here. Just minutes before the drive to the trail head. I feel it, rush to the bathroom and get my confirmation.

It is a sort of relief, not having to await it any longer – but I'm also wondering, why couldn't I have gotten "it" a few days earlier, when we still had a shower and toilets. "Deal with it", am I thinking as I prepare myself to leave. I quickly browse the store for some hygiene products and am happy I didn't get the period only the next day. Back at the trail, there's a whole bunch of hikers walking with us, one by one.

Slowly but surely the pain in my lower area increases. I've never been a big fan of fighting it with medicine. I'm taking a big sip of water and tell you I won't be able to keep up a high pace today. We lose track of the hiking group very fast and walk our own set speed. The guilty conscience gets to me and only increases the intensity of the pain.

The distance between each break becomes shorter and the backpack doesn't really help in making the hike feel like a casual stroll. I now do make the decision to pop a pill. Also to just keep up with the group and not arrive too late at the camp. You're very grateful for my decision.

I had to think for a while before deciding to actually write about the issue of the period. Ultimately, I drew the conclusion that this topic concerns half the population and surely it must be of interest to some readers, possibly some men, too, how you'd survive those days.

I have to say I've never had strong bleedings which was a blessing for the hike. But I had also laid off the pill about a year before which now I was a little upset about. I could've just kept popping the pill.

Either way, two months into the trail am I now having to face this reality. Already ahead of the journey, I started to get acquainted with the menstruation cup. I found it to be the cleanest option for nature and I got some time to prepare dealing with it at the trail later on. Regardless, I did buy some emergency tampons at that small store in Kennedy Meadows, just in case I wouldn't be able to handle the "LadyCup". Whoever knows me, especially you, knows, that I rather be safe than sorry, that I rather take one surplus roll of toilet paper than one too few.

So here I am, pants down by a small creek. My bottle of water to my left, the Ziploc with clean toilet paper, the bag with used toilet paper and the shovel in front of me.

The sky above me flares up in a red-turning blue and I'm directing my whole attention to my surroundings. Shortly before, we had seen those huge bear marks in the tree and now I'm sitting here. Close to their water source, however with enough distance to avoid polluting the clean water with feces. I'm trying to do business but I'm missing the relaxation I'd very much have liked. The comfortable toilet seat got traded for a cold breeze and lukewarm water to wash hands got replaced by the ice cold river. What I'm missing at the comfortable bathroom back home nonetheless, is this indescribably beautiful view. The mist out here embraces nature, and seemingly freezes it in its veil. I'm squatting down and holding my knees inside this foggy part and even forget why I came here in the first place. I stare at the horizon, browsing through the meadows, woods and all the peaks in the distance that are awaiting our ascent. "How far will it be? Is it just days or even weeks before arriving over there? Oh man, this is so magnificent, I can't wait to be feeling more snow beneath my feet! And check out that sunset. Is there anything more beautiful in this world than being out here, knowing you're surrounded by pure nature for miles and miles?", I'm whispering silently to myself.

A squirrel suddenly appears in front of me and I remember why I got down here in the first place.

I'm quickly finishing up whatever there is left to do at an imaginary toilet. Pulling the pants back up and washing my hands in the river before marching back to the others.

Got going at 7am toward the junction and then walked 2.5 miles off-trail to a parking lot where you'll hitch a ride to Lone Pine – if you're lucky, 21 miles away.

After a curvy 30 minute ride, we arrived 6.000ft down at around 100°F. First things first, we had breakfast, beer, a shower and, as expected, did stay for the night by the pool with beer.

DAY 69   06/06/2019   MILE 745 - 753 (+2,5 BACK TO THE PCT)

This morning we already woke up at 5:45am and had breakfast at 7am. A super sweet trail angel couple gave us a ride at 9am back to the trail. Emptied the beers quickly, ate an orange and it's back up to the trail that we reached 2 hours and 2.5 miles later through deep snow.

The PCT was covered no less in snow. We advanced quite slowly and struggled not to sink in (it was usually Finn).

Sadly, my boots aren't exactly 100% waterproof and some water would squeeze in. After 9 hours marching through the snow that is okay, though. I changed my socks occasionally.

We mounted the tents utterly exhausted three miles ahead of the originally scheduled camp spot ... in the snow at 11.264ft ... the hot-water bag is already by Finn's feet :-)

And now, how exactly would you spend a night with snow all around?

Well, the answer is brief: Freezing!

That's just half the truth, however.

Our first night in the snow had not been planned like that. Like previously mentioned, we had wanted to do another 3 miles that day through the snow. But in the afternoon, it turns out to be almost impossible to advance without completely running out of strength through the slushy snow.

We reached the others at the peak, after frequently sinking into the snow all the way to our hips. Totally out of energy are we seeing others mounting their tents already. I'm so excited about this premature camping spot that I scream and feel like the happiest person on Earth – possibly sharing this title with you and the other five fellas.

I look around and all I see is the white, sparkling snow. Our map promises a small lake or river nearby but I can't find it for now. There is a small mountain behind us where the sun is about to set.

We put our backpacks down fast, take the tent out and you start levelling the area where our tent is to be set. You walk in small circles doing tiny steps like a mouse in order to make it plain. I try helping you out but the floor beneath my feet isn't really moving. You keep going as I leave to look for the "lost" water source.

I reached it quickly, hidden beyond a small mountain of snow. I'm slowly approaching the edge of the water. Slowly squat and trying to reach out for the water, unable to reach it though.

You had watched me from away. Certainly, to ensure me not tripping and falling into the water. And here you are, running to me with a pot.

"So, you can't reach the water?", are you asking with a smirk. I'm smiling, leaving you to it and disappear behind a tree.

Tent is mounted, food about to be served, am I leaning back, enjoying the view and let me thoughts roam freely.

DAY 70   06/07/2019   MILE 753 - 767   (+1 MEILE TOWARDS MT. WHITNEY)

Got up at 6am and squeezed our stuff into the backpacks before putting on our frozen boots. Finn's feet were super cold and he had to put down some foot warmers into his shoes which didn't really help much, though. After managing to pull out our hiking sticks from the ice which we had used to replace tent pegs, we got going and warmed up quickly.

Until 8:30/9am, marching through the snow was a blast ... then it turned too wet and slushy.

We were to face our first river crossings in the Sierra. The first one was across a tree trunk, the second one: Shoes off and through f***ing cold water. Three friendly groundhogs were expecting us on the other side. At the junction, "Dumbo" left us because he had done Whitney before already. We marched a mile toward the ascent, which we'll do tomorrow at 2:00/2:30am ...

DAY 71   06/08/2019   (15 MILES)   MT. WHITNEY SUMMIT

Left the camp at 2:30am and walked through darkness with lamps on our heads. It were 4 miles to the foot of the mountain before having a crazy ascent in super deep snow. Equipped with the ice axe and crampons we climbed the almost 80° mountain step by step. Afterwards, it was alongside the cliff with occasionally half a foot of space to walk on. In the end, it was another really steep ascent up to the summit, where we had a breathtaking (literally) view from 14.505ft. The weather was on our side – just perfect! We quickly took a group picture and put down our names at the register before hustling back down, as the snow started to melt. The descent, too, was very exhausting and quite slippery. Once we had mastered some of the altitude and were back down, we enjoyed the great weather and practiced falling down as well as self-rescuing with the ice axe' help. That was fun and you'd rush downhill really fast. As much as we were fighting the heat on our way back, Finn had struggled with the cold that same morning. He had to switch socks half way up and his feet were all blue. In the end, it was an amazing but no less dangerous and exhausting ascent and descent and we're all relieved to be back at the camp alive.

Mt. Whitney. California's highest mountain, also in the US if excluding Alaska, at an altitude of 4.421 meters. Three men named Charles Begole, A. H. Johnson and John Lucas were the first to conquer the mountain back in 1873.

There are no technical difficulties to master if you are to climb the mountain in summer without snow. It's just a long way full of curves leading to the top. However, the climb does require a solid stamina in order to handle the absolute altitude as well as the differences in altitude.

So much for the theoretical part.

We had tons of snow and no actual path, which turned the entire operation into the adventure of climbing an ice wall.

Man, how proud we were once we made it.

But also really stupid!

It wasn't just the crazy descent, but also already during the ascent when we realized the adventure we were going for. A single step could have led into certain death by falling off the cliff at horrendous speed! Some rocks pop out the snow here and there, possibly giving you support as you slide down the cliff – not the ideal support to crash into as you fall. Later on, some hikers tell us they encountered falling rocks when they ascended. They only saw sparks flaring up, nothing more. They first thought to have seen some fellow hikers' lamps. But it was debris coming downhill to cause the sparks. Thankfully, they were not in the way. A few days later we learned that a man was reported missing. His car was parked at the other side of the ascent – and the owner, gone. Then the news hit that a male corpse was found close to the mountain's ascent.

That does happen occasionally. Many adventurous people lose their lives out in nature, they simply disappear.

Already back at San Jacinto Peak we'd see posters of missing people. Sometimes they'd be one or two years old without encountering a single trace.

The beautiful snow may turn into a treacherous fatality.

We were aware of this danger from the very beginning, but nature ate up all our conscience for this risk.

DAY 72   06/09/2019   MILE 767 - 774   (+1 MILE)

We were still really exhausted and left the camp only around 8am, but to merely face some 8 miles that day. It wasn't too bad to have this rather short passage after the previous ascent and the planned crossing of Forester Pass! I saw my first coyote strolling around down a forest clearing. We had some more river crossings but only had to walk through one, whereas the remaining ones were able to be passed via snow bridges or tree trunks. Quite early at the camp spot, we had to find a spot for the night without snow. We hit the sac early (6pm) in order to gather sufficient sleep for "Forester".

DAY 73   06/10/2019   MILE 774 - 787   (FORESTER PASS)

We left almost at the scheduled hour of 3:45am. Again, equipped with lamps on our heads and this time with backpacks fully loaded toward Forester Pass. After two hours, we reached the foot of the mountain. The ascent to the first switch backs was rather steep and exhausting. But we were prepared, for we had done Mt. Whitney just two days before. The switch backs were partially covered in snow and some parts were so narrow that we were forced to climb along the rocks. The ice axe did well in pulling ourselves up. Shortly before the highest part of the pass, we had to cross a slope that was completely covered in snow. The "way" consisted of other hikers' footprints. Step by step, fully concentrated, we managed to cross the path. We all made it and nobody slid down those 600ft. Afterwards, it was just a few more switch backs before reaching the PCT's highest point (13.501ft) – during the biggest snow year ever (2019)!
The other side welcomed us with a huge snowy landscape and a comparatively easy descent down the valley. On our ways to the camp spot, we passed scenic rivers. We had

lunch on arrival at the camp at 12:45pm. Before napping, Finn jumped into the icy river, accompanied by "Doc". Had some more food by the fire at 5pm before it's bed time again at 7pm.

DAY 74   06/11/2019   MILE 787 - 788   (+ 8 MILES TO THE PL)

After merely one mile, we left the PCT toward Kearsarge Pass and the parking lot, from where we would hit Independence/Bishop.

The ascent to the pass was exhausting and I was troubled with breathing problems again. The descent was wet and slippery due to the soft snow.

Once we got to the parking lot, we had to wait for 1.5 hours before we were taken all the way to Bishop by a trail angel named Dennis, where we met the rest of our trail family. Firstly, we took a shower and did laundry before meeting many known faces.

We needed an entire day to hike off the PCT. Marched through snow and ice, along a lake and over a pass, slid down icy slopes and wandered across fields of rocky debris. Only to arrive down in the desert at 100°F and realizing how far off we really were from civilization for the past few days.

"Mr. Mee Too" never told us his real name. Instead, he'd expose his unique character through his lifestyle.

We didn't have much time getting to know each other. "Feathers" had introduced him to us the morning we were off to the High Sierra. Over pancakes and coffee he explained us his compass and how to use it. He hikes exclusively by map and compass.

His hat sits above his ears, pushing them to form some sort of flappy ears. He is of a rather stocky shape, revealing his small beer belly as his short legs find support in chunky boots. I feel like his boots were never really tied, always making me feel uneasy whenever I glanced at them. You felt uneasy by the sight of his chaotically arranged backpack.

Since he had a very special way of speaking and thoroughly enjoyed to express knowing better, we usually kept away from him whenever possible.

It was clear from early on he'd leave the trail around Bishop in order to see his girlfriend, so the acquaintance was kept brief.

We also met "Bambi" on our kick-off day to the Sierra. Short, dark hair and a rather manly appearance through her oversized shirt and loose shorts over her Long Johns. Her incisors are mildly tilted to the front which, however, doesn't derogates her looks. She is an easy-going person to hike with, but we didn't really talk much. That's not due to her teeth but really because it's super exhausting to cross the Sierra. She, like me, enjoys a lowered walking pace. So the group slowed down because of us and relieved us from the pressure to keep up.

DAY 75+76   06/12 - 06/13/2019   ZERO DAYS BISHOP (AT 100°F)

Took the bicycles to Von's and had a delicious breakfast. Checked out the outfitters and picked up our mail. Met Jaja and Tyler again who checked in at the same hostel. We wanted to go bowling at night but there were no free lanes.

Prior to that, we shared nice potato dinner with "Sunshine". The next day we just forwarded our mail and finally met Ben "Sir Loin" again. A quick burger and the best fries ever at the brewery before hitching a ride back to the trail. We got lucky after 1.5 hours and trail angel got us back on track. On arrival, we made a fire and roasted the dough Finn had prepared back at the hostel – with cheese and avocado, insanely good!

DAY 77   06/14/2019   MILE 788 - 789   (AN ENTRY BY FINN)
            (+ 8 MILES FROM THE PARKER ACROSS KEARSARGE)

At 5:20am up to the pass. Met many known faces on our way ("Cheeks" & "Trouble", "Macarena") but also new ones: Björn "Viking" from Kiel. After some chitchat and "rescuing" an elder hiker (around 65yrs) we arrived timely at the camp. Had a nap before sharing lunch altogether at noon, hung our food into the trees and now off to bed. It's 8pm right now and the sun sets slowly. The alarm will ring at 3:45am!

"Heeeey Macarena, ay! ..."
Gently swinging the hip toward the North. Or something like that. We didn't see Justus, his real name, dance too often. But when he was in a good mood, he wouldn't mind stepping up the dance.

His floppy sun hat and a dog patch up front, combined with some short – really short! – sporty pants and a brightly colored fanny pack made him easy to be remembered.

Back home in Germany he is a trained cook and dog trainer,

lives in Berlin but originally comes from the North, hence no accent whatsoever.

He has the gift of the gab and enjoys telling stories.

Our morning was enriched by his story how to raise and educate dogs in order to live in harmony. You were so eager to listen and had all sorts of questions. You wanted to know it all as we really want to get a dog. And just like that, 20 miles are gone.

All I can say about the couple "Cheeks" and "Trouble" is that they are really sweet people we'd run into every now and then on our first part of the trail. Kennedy Meadows South at "Grumpy Bear" was one of the spots, where they had started to work because they were waiting for a package. Him, American, Her, English – I don't recall who was "Cheeks" and who was "Trouble" by now.

And then there is Björn "Viking". Like you wrote in your entry, we got to know him while passing Kearsarge Pass. Coming right toward us with a man in his mid-60s. Quite up at the trail, on a snow-free part, we get to know him a little more. He tells us how he is from Kiel and gives the older man just company until they part ways before headed through the Sierra. Certainly a smart move, not to expose that man further to the Sierra. He keeps slipping in the snow and advances the ascent only really slowly.

"I'll help him move upward. I can't bear the sight of this", are you saying and put down your backpack.

It takes a while for you to reach him further down, but despite utter exhaustion, the man expresses his gratitude in full ease. Since you carry his backpack, he now ascents way faster.

He is fully snorting as he reaches the peak of the pass and promises not to head back into the Sierra but instead to skip this part of the PCT.

We crossed Glen Pass early in the morning. The ascent was quite alright. Once on top, we had a small snack break and walked alongside the slope toward the valley. We were happy to leave this stretch behind as the snow was on the verge of sliding downhill. A long descent followed all the way down to Woods Creek, which we reached via a rope bridge.

We had to cross a few rivers and creeks on our 2-mile way up to Rincho Pass. The last to cross was White Fork Creek. Two boys had crossed already and three girls were waiting with us on the other side. This stream's current was so extreme that we didn't know how to cross. "Horse" and "Feathers" had checked it out further down, but nothing really. We brainstormed as a group how to get to the other side – with a rope, via a trunk ... but the current was too strong! Suddenly, "Horse" walked into the river and the boys on the other side reached out for his hand to pull him out. Followed by "Mr. Me Too", then it was "Feathers'" turn. When Bambi stepped up, the danger had even worsened. The current pulled her feet away before "Feathers" and the others could reach her hand in the last second. That's when Finn and I realized we're definitely not going through that.

The ranger we had previously met had warned us of this crossing which is notorious to force hikers into turning around. The other girls and we were contemplating to detour the entire river somehow. But suddenly they were about to cross the river right there. And then it was just "Sunshine", Finn and I. The last girl affirmed our doubts to avoid crossing – shortly before reaching the other side, she got rocked away by the stream and out of pure luck was pulled on land by the others. This idea wasn't thought through, too hasty and actually not smart at all.

Eventually, we decided to camp by the river. Finn and "Sunshine" walked alongside the stream for two hours looking for a better path to cross it. I was watching our stuff and food when they came back to tell me about snow bridges they had seen leading over the river. Also, the river wouldn't be as dangerous and big over there. We had leftover bread by the fire before going to bed way too late at around 8:30pm.

"I promised to your grandpa to take care of you!", was your answer to me saying "Thanks for not making us cross the river."

It's the first time I'm seriously considering to cancel the whole operation. For the first time, the thought to turn around is tempting, when looking at this purely dangerous river.

When witnessing the girls almost drown, I really panicked. I'm still feeling this panic and fear when reminiscing that very day. The river not even as wide, we could have easily had a conversation by it – had its rushing stream not entirely eaten up our voices. The water so clear and beautiful – had it not been stirred up by the massive rocks and trunks. And the nature surrounding the river – so peaceful, if only you ignored the life-threatening hazards posed by the river.

Two years before, 2017, the PCT's hikers had another year of major snowfall. A young woman named "Strawberry" drowned in one of these rivers.

So can you learn from other people's mistakes? No! Because you can't figure out the trail. We all can just equip ourselves the best way possible, prepare ourselves well, not walk alone, think straight and know how to act in case of emergency. Ultimately, however, we're entirely subjected to nature's will.

Nobody asks you to walk this path. You walk it for yourself. Nobody forces you to be out here. It's entire your call and nobody will lay down a paved road in front of you – you'll have to fight for it. At the end, you emerge from this hike fully loaded with life experience.

DAY 79   06/16/2019   MILE 801 - 804   (+ 3 MILES AROUND
                                                        THE RIVER)

The plan was to walk up the river for 1.5 miles, over the rocks and crossing the river at a safe passage.
5:30am was the kick-off.
We arrived further up easier than expected. We took the first snow bridge, because in case of breaking through the steps, the current still would have been too strong to handle. The river got narrower and the current's intensity weakened.
We laid down a trunk over the snow as additional support. After a little snack, it was back down toward the trail. Refilled our water supply on the other side and were back on the PCT. Quite worn out we decided not to do Pincho Pass but to catch up with our group first. Went to bed around

11:30 at some snow-free spot.
"Master Braider" & the gang are just 1.5 miles behind us ...

Just when we were ready, a group equipped with head lamps came toward us. "Master Braider", Margerite, Parker & the other fellas. All together we headed toward Pincho Pass. This ascent was surprisingly easy, because it wasn't as steep but more of a horizontal ascent. Once back down in the valley, it was river crossings all over again. Snow bridges aided in crossing the river at all times except for South Fork Kings River.

100ft up there was a big trunk enabling us to cross one by one. At the last snow bridge crossing, Parker slipped through a broken step all the way up to his arms. Finn quickly jumped to him and pulled him out. We mounted our tents two miles ahead of Mather Pass on rocks that peaked out of the snow. Just in time, before hail fell. There is occasional hail right now, but it's sleeping time anyway (5:10pm).

Had a stormy night. The ice axe got torn out despite being fixed with ropes. Another rope tore and we had stuck a hiking stick through the tent to avoid it breaking in. At some point, the storm faded.

We left super tired at 5am toward Mather Pass. At the bottom of the ascent we were to decide: Ascending to the left or to the right?

The trail was supposed to lead us to the right. But there were barely any footprints and some avalanches had come down. Thus, we followed the other groups that had advanced already.

It's super steep and we're having to climb over massive rocks and stones to reach the next field of snow. Finn, always 15ft ahead of me, suddenly fell into a snow hole. It all happened so fast that I was just able to grab his backpack, hoping he wouldn't sink in all the way. Half way in, half way down the slope, Finn carefully put down his backpack in order to hoist himself back up.

Back on his feet and we all were relieved. We continued with our legs a little shaky before finally reaching the pass after 15-20 minutes. Then we had a lunch break with a stunning view over the valley, where we'll sleep tonight. Shortly afterwards, we descended on a snow-free curvy pass that was flooded with waterfalls. This gives us an idea of what the Sierra is like in years with less snow – also there are tons of mosquitos.

One day, one pass. Forester first, then Glenn, then Pincho and then Mather. Every day a different mountain pass, a different challenge none of which equals the other and another dozen more to follow.

Forester is the king amongst the passes. Everyone talks about it and fears it.

To climb the highest point of the PCT indubitably is no child's play. But in times of by far the worst year of snow it's a whole different story. The snow up here poses an unforeseen new challenge. There are no longer visible paths to follow and you're fully relying on other hikers' footprints that may either fade within seconds or suddenly lay down various options before you.

This year, however, Mather Pass is the most difficult one by far. It's where you're forced into detouring completely as the regular trail has become unusable due to an avalanche. We're having to climb up the rocks with all our equipment, with crampons to our boots and obviously without any safety measures. The steps merely consist of previous hikers' footprints where you can never tell whether they'll support you sufficiently.

But regardless of the pass we are about to master that day, it's always the same story of getting up super early in order to reach the peak before the sun has risen above the horizon!

You wake up and dress as warm as possible, given the few clothes you're carrying. Pack your stuff, put on the backpack and head lamp and get going to the mountain's foot in plain darkness. This early the snow is covered with a thin layer of ice, letting you advance fairly fast. The group keeps your pace up and nobody wants to slow down the group – hence I'm stepping it up.

I'm walking and barely notice my digestive system to have cranked up already, too. It's not until half way up, highly focused at a steep cliff, carefully doing step by step in slow-motion, that I notice the blatant absence of anything remotely resembling a spot to do business.

For some reason I manage to equilibrate body and mind in this situation and entirely shift my attention to focus properly. I breathe calmly and keep my sight off the cliff. Feeling the cold breeze on my sweat-covered neck. Actually, I'm completely out of breath but I force myself to stay focused and carefully do small steps by the cliff. Every single step is like advancing on a staircase built with steps that are way too large. Requiring my every step to use all my legs' energy to elevate myself and the backpack. My thoughts are completely blank.

After hours of tremendous physical and psychological toll, you reach the peak and forget all the pain you endured in a heartbeat. You're up here, watch the view and embrace the world you're looking down on and that you have conquered with the sheer use of willpower and stamina.

Sadly, I have no kids yet and therefore can't draw parallels to birthing a child. But the conquest of a mountain pass all in the deepest snow possibly resembles the intensity.

DAY 82   06/19/2019   MILE 826 - 836

The first five miles took us through an indescribable fairy tale valley that made me tear up. Just magical!
We passed forests through which rivers ran and where lakes had evolved. Smaller creeks flooded the PCT and deer were grazing in meadows. A small groundhog creeped up to us when we were having a lunch break and out of nowhere started nibbling Alice "Master Braider's" stuff.
Since walking in the Sierra, we're seeing these cute little and trusting fellas almost on a daily basis. Also saw two snakes, I believe they were racers. We decided to camp cowboy-style three miles ahead of the Muir Pass, as we were all utterly depleted.

Cowboy-camping 101: Camping without a tent! Roll out your mattress, put down your sleeping bag and sleep with your valuable stuff inside the sleeping bag.

This sort of camping is the quickest and easiest if you're willing to abstain from a tent.

Many hikers choose this style to advance quickly with light weight through Oregon. A state known for few rainy days in summer. In turn, it'll suck big time should there be rain.

Mile 2.095, you and I completely soaked in the tent. The sun has gone an hour ago and you quickly mounted our tent whilst it was raining cats and dogs. I was inside already organizing our stuff.

The rain drops heavy on the tent and I hear you digging a ditch. Tiny creeks have emerged on the plains we and three other hikers have put their tents on.

Equipped with head lamps and raincoats and the rainfall it was hard to make up the other tents. So we were happy to find a small empty spot on an even surface. I open our backpacks and am happy to see our dry sleeping bags. Thank god we had decided on the waterproof bags back in the day. Everything else is just soaked. I take everything out and arrange space for you and me.

"Come on in quickly, I'm done in here for now. You're getting super wet!", I'm yelling at the rain.

"Larissa, I'm completely wet already, like it can't get any worse! I can take my time now."

I'm laughing.

"Watch out, coming in now", are you shouting and I'm opening the tent's zipper of the mosquito net.

Head first, with the hair all dripping and then your body – throwing yourself on your side inside the tent. Your feet are still outside when you realize a small puddle has joined us in the tent already. You quickly take off your blue shirt, the colorful shorts, your underwear and socks – you're wet, cold and naked, just sitting there.

You're looking at me crestfallen and apparently blank. I'm laughing "I have nothing for you to dry yourself off with. Maybe try my Bandana."

Fortunately, we stored our spare clothes in the dry bag, too, enabling you to not be hiking naked the next day. Surely, with 100% humidity nothing will dry until the coming morning.

We take out our cooking tools when there is a sudden "knock" at the door.

"Hello?", are we wondering.

"Hello?!"

"Hi, I don't have a tent and all my stuff got wet. Do you have any more room in your tent for me?"

I raise my eyebrow and look at you, shaking my head.

"What's wrong with your tent? Do you have a tarp?", are you asking him.

"Yes, I have a tarp, but it's not big enough and my sleeping bag got wet and I'm cold"

You roll your eyes and I'm whispering to you: "No way will he sleep in here! He can join us for as long as we're eating but he'll definitely not sleep between us like a baby."

"It's very small in here and everything in here is wet, too. What about the others, do they have some room for you?"

"No, I asked them already."

You sigh and respond "Ok. Come in then, but it's super tight in here!"

We open the tent and yet another waterfall unleashes onto you. Head first and then his body. Apart from a few drops on his shirt he enters completely dry, carrying a rain coat in his hand. I offer him the spot on the opposite side where he gets comfortable right away. I'm asking him to keep his feet, covered in mud, outside in the vestibule.

And here we are – us, soaked, him, dry – diving into a conversation about ourselves and our prior hike. He tells us he started in Cascade Locks four days ago and is about to go southbound through Oregon – without a tent.

The next day we learn from other hikers that he turned around, canceled the trip and didn't go anymore South.

That has nothing to do with "hiker porn" though!

Back to mile 836 and the stone where we wanted to cowboy-camp on. The sky was painted blue, the sun high up and we were chatting, lying on our sleeping bags. We had to establish the tent early into noon like every day in the Sierra due to the snow being too muddy to keep going. We were so close to just keeping up the hike in order to reach the Muir Pass where we'd have one of the rare huts to sleep in. But destiny chose different and here we are, enjoying ourselves burning in the sun in the middle of a snow field. We're surrounded purely by mountains and white-sparkling icy crystals.

It's time to get out the food bags and recounting the stash once again, always hoping the recounting would magically multiply the remaining food. Hunger is your constant companion and usually triumphs over all other thoughts, leading your mental way.

No surplus food! We're exchanging, though. You're sick of your cereal bars and Margerite of her cookies. "Sunshine" invites everyone to gummy bears and you're enriching people's lives with "Tom Kah".

Suddenly, amidst our chatting, a huge bang in the distances echoes to us. Our heads turn toward the mountain and we see it: A massive field of snow loosens and breaks off the cliff, sliding down the slope at an enormous velocity. A gigantic cloud of snow blows toward the sky and an avalanche rushes downhill.

With our heads supported by our hands we are in safe distance to witness this natural spectacle and a new term arises: "Hiker porn"

DAY 83   06/20/2019   MILE 836 - 850

Woke up early and the sleeping bags were entirely wet. There was no rain, it was "just" the dew.
3 Miles to Muir Pass, without the ice axe. Up at the hut we met some 20 other hikers and it was quite cozy inside. Afterwards, we rushed down until finally encountering a dry spot to dry up our sleeping bags.
Our second river crossing that day was at mile 850 which was the biggest one, thus far. Waist-deep in the current, I

held tight onto Finn's backpack for the 60ft crossing. We crossed like this step by step, close to each other. 10 minutes later we found our camp spot. Early enough to dry our stuff still. And we finally had some food by the fire.

DAY 84   06/21/2019   MILE 850 - 863

The first time in the Sierra to sleep in and we left the camp only around 8:30am. Walked along Evolution Creek for a while and then further down the valley. We picked some onions on our way and really stepped it up a notch when finding out that there is a hiker box loaded with tons of food at the Muir Trail Range. Took some snacks and food for 1-2 dinners before it was steep up back to the PCT for "only" 0.5 miles as we had to leave the trail in order to reach the range. Another 3 miles before we all were quite tired and really enjoying our new dinner.
PS: Today was National-Hike-Naked-Day and Ashes was the only one to make it happen all the way.

DAY 85   06/22/2019   MILE 863 - 879

Today it was time for Selden Pass. The easiest one by far. We encountered some difficulties in the morning in the dark, but the trail led us along the lake when the sun rose. Again, we had some smaller creek crossings. On our way down we passed West Fork Bear Creek that we were supposed to cross twice within one mile. We chose to walk alongside instead and pick an alternative route. "Sunshine" and Marguerite did want to give it a shot but quickly changed their minds when finding out the danger of the second crossing. We were just about to figure out a way to pass one of the two creeks somehow that were ahead of us on this alternative route. At first, the boys tried laying down a trunk but the current pulled it away in an instant. In the meantime, Alice found a crossing that wasn't too deep and the current not to strong.

We crossed in couples wearing our boots. The second crossing was via a trunk.

It was another ten miles we did being pretty worn out, when deciding to refrain from doing another two miles and instead mount our camp. Everyone is super exhausted.

Tomorrow will be this stretch's last pass.

DAY 86   06/23/2019   MILE 879 - 894   (AN ENTRY BY FINN)

Got going 5 am sharp and had the first river crossing right away. Alice & Marguerite left earlier and Alice fell into the crossing and lost her phone.

Shortly afterwards (uphill the entire morning) the second river crossing. "Sunshine", Parker and us crossed over a log. "Ashes" walked through elsewhere and got torn away: Trekking pole gone!

The third RC at some waterfalls. Larissa got her feet wet, then we hiked upward to Silver Pass. Downhill we were able to slide big time!! Another climb with endless switch backs and then down to Purple Lake where we warmed up by the fire and mounted the tents (camping forbidden).

Catching up some miles, but the snow slows us down and the rivers are doing a number on the group. The time schedule is screwed and every river crossing delays our target by two miles.

My shoes, monotonously, one by one. It's hypnotizing but I'm fully focused.

I raise my head and see yet another river coming at us. This time, it lies peacefully to our feet, like a sleeping child, that will, however, go nuts if you dare waking it up. That's how you occasionally underestimate the rivers, you tumble and lose grip beneath your feet.

Sometimes the river is fully in motion, drawing panic onto your face but with inner tranquility and patience you'll find your safe way through. Hence, every situation requires individual assessment and act according to the circumstances of the crossing.

Trekking poles into the ground, backpack off, shoes off and tied around your neck, backpack back on and poles back into your hands. It's important to keep the lash on your backpack open, in case of tripping to the ground.

I'm feeling the ice cold snow slip into my sandals from the side. Every step is done with care in order to reach the other side as dry as possible.

I find myself before the river, take a deep breath, stick the trekking poles into the river, make up and focus on the way through before putting down the first step into the water.

"Air", am I thinking and desperately breathing in.

My heart starts pounding right away, the breathing pace increases and my body yells at maximum power: "Get out!" I'm withstanding the inner voice and ignore the instincts.

The second foot into the river and that's when I feel it. The water, pressing against my legs and lower body. I'm holding up with all my strength, find support in my hiking sticks and try walking up against the current.

I dare advancing a little step, followed by the other food and my body screams. My feet put their trust into my eyes, because I no longer feel them. I'd love to just run, but instead they move me at snail pace.

I moan, make funny faces and my thoughts halt as it feels like a million needles sting into my legs.

Getting closer to the other side in full focus, seeing you reaching out the hand and I pull myself out.

Made it! Not at all, really! Now it's that the pain really kicks in.

With shaky hands do I open the Velcro on my camp shoes and carefully take them off before releasing a scream. The pain of a knife you're trying to ram into someone's foot. In tears and with great care do I take off my sandals.

And here we are. Crouching down, holding our feet with our hands and not saying a single word.

The water rushes by, the birds are chirping, the bees are buzzing and foliage rustles in the wind.

But I'm not hearing none of it. I feel like in trance, moving forth and back with my body, try to endure the pain and await the moment to feel my feet again.

Seconds and minutes pass before life slowly returns into our blue feet.

The breathing calms down, our senses are sharpening up again and we quickly realize how beautifully nature around us is blossoming and blooming.

We grant ourselves a break, stretch our legs, take out a snack and enjoy a "Cliff Bar".

DAY 87   06/24/2019   MILE 894 - 911

This morning definitely was one of the, if not THE coldest morning. Back in the night we had already felt my sleeping bag getting wet from the outside despite of the tent ... everything else remained dry.

We had an extended breakfast two hours into the hike where everyone dried their tents and sleeping bags. Afterwards, we got closer to those 7.000ft and finally got out of the snow around noon and entered amazing woods. Had to cross a few streams but most of them already had makeshift bridges from trunks built across them already. Passed massive waterfalls before the arrival at the camp.

Tomorrow we're off to Mammoth. *And thus, we chalk off the 900th mile.*

DAY 88 - 90   06/25 - 06/27/2019   MILE 911 - 915 (+ ZERO DAYS)

Last day at the trail before headed back to civilization after 12 days. This morning we rocked the last four miles in 75 minutes. Then we had to walk another 4 miles at a closed road to a skiing resort where we took a bus to town. Since we were early in Mammoth, we easily found a place to stay for all of us. We prepared a nice dinner for the group and played Fishbowl. Had tons of fun that night and went to bed way too late.

The next morning we had "Homemade-Eggs-Florentine"

before resupplying for the upcoming two stretches till South Lake Tahoe. Another gathering for dinner and playing Fishbowl once more.

Today, we wanted to get back on the trail and ran into Tyler, "Snack Pack" and "Sir Loin". Sent the resupplying package to Kennedy Meadows North and then it was four miles road walk back down to the PCT. Made a fire where we enjoyed our leftovers from the AirBnB before we'll continue tomorrow at ease.

DAY 91   06/28/2019   MILE 915 - 926

With our backpacks fully stashed we left at 8am. Everyone feels like they loaded up way more food than last time, because apparently we all had too little food for the last stretch. We advanced only by one mile an hour but were fighting snow again half way into the hike.

All worn out did we arrive at the camp at 5 pm.

DAY 92   06/29/2019   MILE 926 - 942

We overslept full on and got woken up by the others that were set to leave already. They were so nice as to wait for us packing our things within 35 minutes. Didn't have to cross not too many rivers and arrived around 7:30am at the pass. It was a quick way down and the snow was gone again. From there on, it was a cruisy hike, a mild descent along the river toward Tuolumne Meadows. Ran into two rangers checking our permits. Then had a really refreshing bath in the river before a nice lady took us to Yosemite Valley.

Yosemite Valley, the epitome of the beauty of nature and majestic wonders.

We drive along the curvy road and my heart starts pounding, a tingling in my stomach ignites and then I see him – El Capitan. A legend, to literally emerge before us from the grounds. The car's windows are too small to get a full view of him. We're passing him slowly as my eyes are focused on the rocky walls and the climbers that are about to ascent.

He stands 2.307 meters above sea level and is an insane challenge for every climber that face vertical flanks of up to 1.000 meters.

The Nose is one of the most common routes. In 2018, Alex Honnold and Tommy Caldwell, known people in the climbing scene, conquer El Capitan's peak after just two hours.

One more curve down the road, Yosemite Falls, some of the highest waterfalls in the world, surface and behind it there's already "Half Dome".

It feels like the dream lands of a nature-boy, who roams the earth in the conquest of discovering the unknown wherein he passes valleys and mountains and befriends nature.

The truth reveals different, as it is a famous destination in uncounted travel guides to where people from all over the world hustle to. We end up at a traffic jam and see hundreds of people walking by. Old, young, sporty, casual – the tourists' portfolio is on display in its biggest variety. The forest fades behind masses of people and you just want to be back on the PCT.

But what can I say – ultimately, we turn out to be tourists as well. Thus, off into touristic adventures.

Not quite like Alexander and Tommy – but also fully loaded with adrenaline are we carefully advancing over the field of stony debris. It all went so fast leaving us no choice to rethink twice.

We had met Brian and James, two climbers, back down at the parking lot and just like that we find ourselves in their van toward El Cap. Absolutely stunned by the situation, the nicely built bus and all the climbers' gear am I now sensing the beer and "vodkila" rising to my head. I look to you and see you grin like a Cheshire cat. Then "Macarena" catches my attention who looks like he had just fought Cheshire cat. So I felt ambivalent about this interlude adventure.

Out of the bushes and over the field of debris are we now seeing where we stand. Amidst the flanks of El Capitan with a dizzying sight. I immediately push myself against the horizontally arising structure and try not to slip off these tiny steps. I'm still balancing out when seeing the boys proudly present their rope. The very rope we are now to trust with our lives as we are about to push ourselves off the rock.

"Of course! Like I don't mind to die right now.", I'm thinking sarcastically and halt for a second.

I'm monitoring the rope all the way up where it's mounted in the distance at a rock spur.

"Oh, don't worry. Random climbers change that rope every now and then."

"Fantastic, seems like a safe deal.", Macarena turns around to me with sheer panic in her eyes. Again, couldn't overhear the irony in that.

You're immediately defusing the situation by hopping in and offering ever so euphorically to go first after Brian and James.

"Ahhhhhh!", a few minutes later, I can't help but release a fully blown scream. Endorphins explode in surplus and once again I'm completely out of thoughts.

You got hot on that adrenaline feeling and are about to try it again. Strapped in, carabiner mounted, grabbing the rope, startup and go. You swing, float and scream and return with a loud bang to the rocky wall. Not really as cool as you'd like but without unsolicited injuries.

"Alcove Swing" – Our little intermittent adventure.

DAY 93   06/30/2019   ZERODAY   YOSEMITE
                                         VALLEY *RATTLESNAKE ENCOUNTER*

The plan: Climbing Upper-Yosemite-Falls (North America's highest waterfalls) and then having a seat at El Capitan's feet to watch the climbers.

Everyone has just day-trip-backpacks while I stroll with my fanny pack without breaks up the switchbacks, passing the tourists. Feels really cool. On the top, "Horse" invited us to beer and we had butter-Nutella-tortilla. Back down we literally ran and shortly before arrival, we met that one couple that had served us "Vodkila" from their trunk. On the way back, Finn yelled to a van owner "You lost your poptart!" The guy looks from his vehicle and "Sunshine" recognizes his buddy Brian. They're two climbers that took us with them to El Cap and had that idea to do this "Alcove Swing". In utter excitement and fueled with some "Vodkila" and beer, it was upward the El Capitan to the rope for the swing. Brian and James tried first, then it was "Sunshine" and "Macarena's" turn before Finn and I went.

It was awesome! Finn and "Macarena" immediately went for a second round ...

This zero-day really was worth it! Just an insanely beautiful day ... with things adding up just perfectly – simply amazing!

DAY 94   07/01/2019   MILE 942 - 951

Left the valley hitch-hiking and started at the trail around 1:30pm. The journey continued quite cruisy again before hundreds of mosquitos ambushed us just two miles ahead of the camp. It lasted for the rest of the hike. In fact, it were so many we could barely walk straight as we just tried keeping them out of our faces. At the camp, we all jumped into our rain gear and made a fire. The smoke didn't help as much but ultimately our tents saved us.

DAY 95   07/02/2019   MILE 951 - 969

Luckily, this morning we had no more mosquitos and could dive into the day at ease. The first five miles were a piece of cake before encountering that day's first river crossing. Our feet again were hurting badly afterwards and we needed time before feeling our toes again. Only 0.1 miles later there was another river crossing. After a beautiful lunch break by the lake, there were more river crossings coming at us but only the first one made us take off our shoes. The remaining ones could be passed via snow bridges or trunks. Tonight we'll camp at the lake and we're hoping for the night not to be too wet. By the way, we saw a snake eating a fish today.

This morning we heard and saw a woodpecker but when Finn and "Sunshine" were about to listen at the trunk, the little one was already gone. Firstly, it was uphill in the icy snow before going down again and confronting a pretty big river crossing that actually consisted of 4 individual crossings.

We passed Seavey Pass that surprised us with a beautiful ascent before going down on the other side really steep and sketchy on the snow along the river. We had even more river crossings before walking across stone stairs and passing flowers to arrive at today's camp. After eating, had another great view over that Yosemite.

I ran the last "stairs" while you were refilling our water bags. The others are at the top already as they hadn't waited at the river crossing.

"Why haven't you waited for us, at the river crossing? And then left "Sunshine" behind by himself. That's the whole reason why we're hiking together! To help each other and never leave anyone alone"!

You're furious and do not await the group's answer but look for a camping spot far off the group.

The descent steep, the river rapid and the trail alongside the river so narrow that you can barely put your feet next to one another. For now, there is some snow left. The cliff and path are covered and occasionally pieces would break off into the water. "Whooosh" ... Snow eaten by the river and the swift current making it disappear in seconds. Carefully, step by step, we're advancing without any certainty to find support with the next step. We're having to walk around rocks, over bushes emerging from the snow and we keep having to push us out from snow holes into which we plummet.

"What are we going to do if one trips? He'll most definitely drown in an instant!"

This question keeps popping up in my head as much as I keep pushing it away to make way for a clear focus that I'm needing right now.

Shortly afterwards, the group split up. That was not unusual. Everyone at his own pace. Us two usually at the very end.

"Ok, once we're back, we'll put major cash to the side and I'll try to work even more. Now it's just the bachelor's thesis ahead and one class of my choice."

"Well, but how much is a van like that? If we really want to convert it properly and then keep driving it for a few years, I'm sure we're looking at some 7-10 thousand Euros.", I'm responding adult-like.

"Perhaps not this year but as of February I'll be able to work full-time until you finish your master's"

I'm losing myself in calculative thoughts.

"If we're back in September and I'll need another three months, I'll be done by January 2021."

"A three-seating bench upfront would be so sick, we could take another person still."

"Well, five seats wouldn't be too shabby either", am I smiling and winking to you.

"Oh, so you want to keep the bus for that long?", are you responding with a smirk.

"A tent-top would be so rad, too. Like having two sleep on the roof and another three persons inside. Or even better on top of the driver's cabin. The kids will love it ... I mean someone's kids of course."

I burst into laughter.

"I'll definitely need a safe place for our Ute Box from Australia and the fishing gear."

Time flies by and suddenly we stand in front of a river. We're on eye level with some small waterfalls finding its way through the rocks and we can't really see the end. As we're standing there without knowing exactly where to proceed, "Sunshine" suddenly appears out of nowhere. He's sitting on a rock without a backpack like Peter Pan and tells us how to others marched on but he had awaited us to show us the way to cross.

You take the lead as we cross stones covered in algae, slippery branches and flooded rocks. I'm right behind you and keep sliding off. My feet get wet and the current destabilizes my grip. You keep turning around to ensure me keeping up but my velocity slows down.

I freeze.

"I can't do it, the jump is too big", am I yelling against the rushing waters.

138

You reach out your hand but it's too far. Then "Sunshine" grabs your backpack and you walk toward me.

With care are we managing to advance slowly. One last jump and here I am completely exhausted. My breathing tightens, my eyes turn wet and I can't hold back any longer. With my hands covering my eyes am I starting to cry and release all the tension. You hold me in your arms to caress me and little by little do I start to ease up. Keep on! The three of us toward the day's target.

One hour later, we reached today's sleeping spot. Refilling water and arranging the group, mounting the tent, preparing food, eating food, calming down and enjoying the stunning sunset with everyone else.

"Good night, everyone."

DAY 97   07/04/2019   MILE 983 - 1.000

Had a rather big river crossing in the morning. "Macarena" crossed first (without the backpack) to check out the depth and the current. Once she gave the "go", we followed one by one to end up on the other side all stiff in pain. As we were sitting on the other side to deal with the pain, we awaited feelings to come back to our toes. In the meantime, "Macarena" caught a rainbow trout. Then it was off toward Dorothea Lake Pass which was different from the others. Were all pretty worn out when arriving at 5:30pm on top. Yet we chalked off those three miles till the 1.000 mile mark. Whoop whoop!

Sun cups as far as the eye reaches. Those goddamn suckers, why would nature invent them? Leif would respond: "Well that's just how nature created it!"

A fir needle drop, the snow surrounding it melts, a hole forms. This hole keeps melting and the emerging water accelerates that very process. Additionally, the white snow reflects the sun rays inside the hole and shaping it deeper. A structure consisting of thin ice picks arises, with narrow tiny bridges over which we are balancing.

"Fuuuuck, I'm tired of this!", I yell out loud.

Again, I tripped into one of these cone-shaped holes.

"It drains all my energy! Finni, get me out of here, please!", am I begging you whilst knowing very well that you're just as powerless to do anything and just as annoyed.

"Come on, have some nuts, that'll help you. Plus I think it's not that far from here."

I halt, do not move a bit, am without strength. My body screams for energy supply and my feet for a few days of break. I let go and drop into the snow, where I hear … nothing. Silence.

"Hey sweetie, whatchu doing there? Come on up, that's too cold four your little raisin! Please get up!"

I'm still just lying there and watch the sky with an empty glance. No airplane, as opposed to that one movie "Wild". That's where she also looks at the sky and sees airplanes pass – but not now, just blue sky.

My mind empty, and so is the stomach. The energy is used up but the fire isn't gone.

Suddenly I see nuts in front of my eyes. Are nuts able to fly? I'm confused.

"Come on, eat!"

I look into your beautiful brown eyes, as I feel so in love with you, start to smile and say "thank you!"

You are the tinder that will forever fuel my fire! Thank you!

Got going not too early and all left individually toward Kennedy Meadows North. Rather cruisy before reaching the ascent for that day which was completely covered in snow (on top of snow cups). Once on top, we could well see the Sierra lying behind us and Northern California to await us. Very cool!

On the way back down to the highway/Sinorra Pass, the way led down a long snow slide where Finn unexpectedly tripped and slid down at full throttle. He lost both trekking poles and his cap and put down some unsolicited somersaults. I was next and collected his stuff on my way. Down at the highway there was trail magic and a trail angel brought us up Kennedy Meadows Resort. We had to sleep 150ft off the hiker campground because we were unable to find it in the dark.

Only with a mosquito net beneath a million stars

DAY 99   07/06/2019   MILE 1.017 - 1.027

Chilled in KM for a bit and then hitched a ride around noon back to the trailhead. Apart from some snow for 2 hours it was rather easy and we could do another ten miles that afternoon which made us arrive at the camp a little earlier than the previous days. Had (once again) a nice fire.

DAY 100   07/07/2019   MILE 1.027 - 1.051

Left around 6am as we intended to catch up with the remaining group (Parker, "Wrong Way", Rachel) in order to wake them up the next morning with blaring hooters. On our 23.5 miles we had some 30-40% snow and the rest was uncovered. Some minor river crossings but none we had to take our shoes off for. We did, however, lose track a few times in the snow and of course it was always downward, forcing us to climb back up. It's about 2.5 miles we assume to be behind the others and will get up accordingly early ;-) ... Let's see if it works out.

Short, stoned and super funny! "Wrong Way", always a smile on his face, in the best years of his life, which, however, he doesn't look. Well, only if he takes off his hat to reveal the somewhat thin hair. You can have a great time with "Wrong Way" anyway and I guess his trail name doesn't need much of an explanation.

The first time we met ... I don't even recall, he was just there. Didn't mind at all as he simply always multiplies the fun. His talks would always cheer one up and we learned how to enjoy life in a more relaxed fashion. All in all a great companion whose motto was: "Take it easy and no rush."

Rumors of
Northern California

Rumor has it that there won't be snow as of mile 1.050. And a rumor it should remain!

Accept it or fight it, give up or keep going, scream or laugh.

I close my eyes, suck in the fresh cold air. Take a deep breath and feel tiny icy crystals form in my nose. I'm feeling every single one of them like tiny stings of needles. I'm sensing the freshness deep inside, this clear unused air. It floods my longs, opens them up and fills them with pure joy of life.

I crack up, accept the challenge and march on.

It would have been too nice.

Grumpy mode on am I following your steps through the muddy snow.

"I'm sick of this. Snow all day, every day, for weeks, and the end seems everything but close.", I think and pull a long face – even longer than this stretch.

I believe it's all about the attitude. In the beginning and when you learn that there won't be more snow at some point it's like all good. You get used to the idea of facing your white enemy on a daily basis.

Of course, it's hella draining and all but come on, it's all part of the deal and in a way really cool actually. Out of a sudden not really, though. At some point, every spot free of snow gets declared the end of the Sierra and as soon as you realize to have been proved otherwise, you fall into an abnormal snow depression. Just like the mountains – it was a constant up and down of emotions. Mentally almost more exhausting than hiking in the snow itself.

DAY 101   07/08/2019   MILE 1.051 - 1.077   *TRAILMAGIC*

Took off at 4:30am and blew the horn around 5:30am. Sadly we couldn't see their faces but they were awaken right away. :)
Today we only had minor snow patches and we had to bust through snow only like twice. Hence, we pulled off 26.2 miles today and the trail magic by the road (scrambled eggs, fruits, Gatorade, ...) surely did its part. Feet are hurting 14 hours into the hike and we're happy to be in bed.

DAY 102   07/09/2019   MILE 1.077 - 1.090

Were the first ones to leave the camp at 5:30am and once again roamed through fantastic landscapes toward South Lake Tahoe. Until the last moment we had hoped to chalk off the last miles without snow – just to find ourselves fighting through snow until 2 miles ahead of the highway.

Hitched a hike pretty fast on arrival. Once in town, we sadly had to find out that the sushi restaurant we had conquered 26 miles for was closed for that very week. Too bad.

DAY 103   07/10/2019   ZERO-DAY   SOUTH LAKE
                                               TAHOE

Got up "early", had breakfast and then strolled to town looking for a bug net, board shorts, new socks and food. Shopping always takes up so much of our time that we managed to send our mail (including a bear can) only at 5pm. Back at the hostel, "Macarena" and Rachel convinced us to stay for another night. We had curry for dinner.

DAY 104   07/11/2019   MILE 1.090 - 1.108   *BEAUTIFUL
                                                 LAKE ALOHA*

This morning 7pm sharp, a trail angel drove us back up the PCT. So sweet. Had a quick coffee 2 miles into the hike at Echo Lake before leaving in trail runners without spikes, a bear can and gaiters. After a minor brunching break, we got off the wrong path for like 20 minutes before noticing it and having to walk all the way back. Later on it was crossing Dicks Pass and we mounted the tent at the lake around 7:30pm.

Barefoot, here I am, feeling the cold coming from the stone I'm standing on. Feeling, how the stone structure stings into my naked feet. We're not having this bare sensation too often out here as we are way too scared to damage our feet, rendering us unable to keep going. The feet are absolutely crucial, they carry you for all these miles. Watch them and take good care of them! Hence, I now am really enjoying this moment of freedom I am able to grant my feet. I'm feeling them breathe as I stand watching the sun set and take a deep breath myself.

Closing the eyes one more time and noticing the last sunrays on my skin.

I sit down, grab my small feet and monitor them carefully. Not too much to notice, covered in sand, dirt and sweat – just after one day – and it'll be a few more days before being able to wash them again. Apart from that they appear just fine. I can just overlook the few smaller blisters and no inflammations whatsoever. Quite the opposite in your case.

I get down in front of you, put your foot on my lap and closely look at your heels before slowly tearing off the tape of the back of your foot. Despite being super careful, the soaked, soft skin gets peeled off piece by piece as it just sticks to the tape. Bare, wet, fleshy skin emerges. You're making a face but keep quiet. Bloody and slobby liquid runs off your heel. I carefully blot it.

Now about to check out your little toe.

"I'll cut it off! Who needs this one anyway and then I'll be pain-free! I'll look it up whether it's possible."

The little toe has swollen up to twice its normal size and looks like the blister-liquid is about to burst.

"Should I sting it open? We don't want this to inflame!"

"Go for it! Get that shit out, it hurts so bad. But disinfect the needle first."

After having poked open the blister and mopped it up, I'm slowly starting to clean up your big toe and disinfect as well. A few minutes later your toe is visible and the inflamed, ingrown toe nail comes up. Using a nail file to remove the dirt that is stuck beneath the nail and try to be as careful as possible. As you lie down on your back, it's tough for you to bear the pain whenever I accidentally touch the inflammation. I feel so sorry for you, but the cleaning process every evening does help and it appears to be less swollen. Applying some disinfecting spray, zinc cream and a band-aid – putting on socks and then off to bed.

DAY 105   07/12/2019   MILE 1.108 - 1.131   *BEAUTIFUL LAKE ALOHA*

Sleeping in for once! Alarm clock would go off at 5am already but we didn't get up until 7am. After two minor ascents, it was downhill for seven miles. We were able to keep up our 3-mile-target (3 miles per hour) thanks to our trail runners that enabled us just simply marching through the creeks. The entire day we saw just one other hiker – plus a bunch of horses with their riders.

Tonight one of the best camp spots ... regarding the view ... but tons of mosquitos.

DAY 106   07/13/2019   MILE 1.131 - 1.153

The snow isn't over by far! And there are more and more mosquitos! This combination at a path downhill covered in snow isn't really ideal. We were really caught up by the snow and yet we made it all the way to the skiing resort with our feet hurting. Down there, we had beer & burger.

"Hiker trash" – the same amount of backpacks and people. Some lost-looking day hikers in between. The smell of food gets to you from afar – and with it, a somewhat stingy beer odor.

"Hey, there you are."

"Cool, you did it!"

"Nice to see you guys."

"Didn't expect you hiking that far."

"Yeah, you made it."

There they are, crammed together like sardines in a can – loaded with beers and burgers in their hands and yelling at us in pure joy. Cheering and looking like they haven't seen a shower in years. Resembling poor, street-living, worn-out creatures but all while having the biggest smiles ever on their faces. Hard to recognize in the men though, as they're all covered in full grown messy beards. The sparkle in their eyes tell the whole story though.

The faces are tanned and covered in dust and sweat. The clothes have turned into one equal mash of earth colors; only a second glance would give a hint as to their original color. They're torn, hanging off in pieces and show traces of salt due to the sweat. The shoes sport additional manmade holes and are fixed with tape.

Backpacks are lining up at the wall of the small wooden shack. In front of them are tons of caps, jackets, sleeping backs, mattresses tents, filters, bottles, phones, power banks, cookers, food, pots, spoons, socks and shoes.

Dirt, sweat, mud, salt, sand, ground and blood are representative of all the miles that have been achieved. They tell stories – the stories that are being shared at the tables by hikers with their mouths full.

"Hi, where are you hiking to?"

"Canada, bro.", you're responding.

"Haha funny. Good joke, man. Have a good day!"

There he goes, laughing along the way. We look at each other, shrug and burst into laughter.

DAY 107   07/14/2019   MILE 1.153 - 1.175

After having the alarm clock snoozing for a solid 1.5 hours, we finally managed to get up.

Today, it was a lot of ups and downs! The ascents were without troubles, downward we'd usually pushed through snow. Hopefully it'll be done by Sierra City (Or so says "Watermelon").

We're not as tired as yesterday and go to bed with the sun still up at 8:15pm.

4 miles before reaching the camp, Finn had gotten stung by a bee, but gladly his foot didn't swell.

DAY 108   07/15/2019   MILE 1.175 - 1.202   *HERO-TIME*

6am straight we left toward Sierra City where we had to check in the latest by 4:30pm as the store would close at 5pm.

Our target (or the attempt) was 10 by 10am and 20 by 2pm. We achieved it by a few minutes, as we had a bigger lunch break (45 minutes) and a drinking break (20 minutes). As it was so hot on the way up to the 4.500ft, we didn't reach our 20 by 2pm goal.

We arrived at the road at 2:45pmand immediately hitched

a ride from a nice lady. 3.5 hours of resupplying, eating, charging the power bank and a cold shower.

Then we decided to actually go back to the trail and did another 7 miles and 2.800ft of altitude before it got dark. Tomorrow we'll sleep in!

DAY 109   07/16/2019   MILE 1.202 - 1.224

Slept in really nicely ... got kissed by the sun at 7am and got back at the hike at 9am. Today, we felt that we're finally off the icy altitudes and we do have to stock up our electrolytes supply. Had a major lunch break at 2pm with mac & cheese and finished off with a little nap. That turned on us big time, as we felt so bloated on the hike and got tired quickly. As opposed to the scheduled arrival time of 6pm, we didn't reach the camp spot until 8:30pm. Shortly before, we saw a deer lurking in the shadows of the trail before getting closer to us all trustingly. Eventually, it did run off.

DAY 110   07/17/2019   MILE 1.224 - 1.250   (AN ENTRY BY FINN)

Woke up with deer by our tent and got going quickly. No snow! It was super hot instead which we gladly accepted. Had aimed to do 21 miles.

Now, after 26 miles and cooling down in the river, dinner with "Midnight Joke" and his girlfriend by the fire, we are dead tired in the tent.

DAY 111   07/18/2019   MILE 1.250 - 1.268

Had a fairly steep and long ascent this morning. Took off around 7am and reached the peak at noon. Finn's shirt was dripping with sweat and even I for once came up with some sweat patches. Up there, we had a full-blown 3.5 hour break as the sun was beating down today. Then it was just another 7.5 miles before mounting our tents. Met "Dumbo" again by the way. Who had been waiting for 2 hours to hitch a ride by the road.

DAY 112   07/19/2019   MILE 1.268 - 1.287   *BELDEN*

Except for a short ascent of 3.5 miles, it was basically downward only, also with a heavily steep so my knees would hurt after a short while. Once we reached Belden around 3pm, we went to get burgers, fries and a milkshake at the RV park Caribou Crossroad. It was followed by the usual procedure of taking a shower, washing and getting food for the next stretch. We slept at the North Forks Feather River and got woken up numerous times by passing trains.

DAY 113   07/20/2019   MILE 1.287 - 1.301

After a nice and relaxed breakfast, we worked our way up from about 2.200 ft to about 7.100 ft in the midday heat. For a long time we have also seen a rattlenake and the number of mosquitoes increased. When we arrived at the top, we were greeted by a couple of "almost missed" Snow Patches. Protected from mosquitoes, we enjoy the sunset with Mac&Cheese =)

Yesterday someone told us there is "Trailmagic" at the Humbold Rd, so we got up early, very excited and did the 10 miles quickly without much food and indeed... beer, Cola, sandwiches, biscuits, fruit and much more... *Trailmagic*

We spend about 2 hours there before we hit the trail again ... Our goal: Soldier Creek about 16 miles further. But before we arrived at the creek in pitch black (around 9:30/10 am), we already had the beer we brought with us and dinner at the "Halfway Marker". Half of the PCT is done!

Halfway Mile Marker

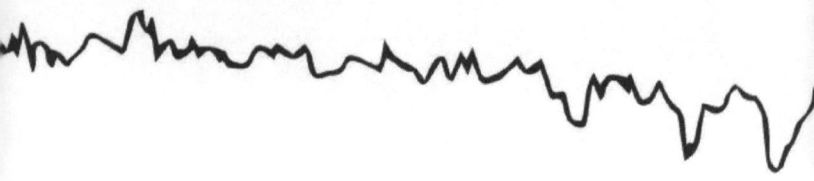

"And into the forest I go, to lose my mind and find my soul."

- John Muir -

We really had been excited for this moment and imagined how we'd feel and in which condition we'd find ourselves in.

Half the Pacific Crest Trail now lies behind us. We've hiked 1.323 miles and casually strolled for a whole 3.549.610 steps. Needed 114 days and ascended 239.707ft of altitude to be followed by 240.362ft of descent. Crossed dozens of passes, fought our way through rivers so many times, stood our ground to the heat and easily conquered our swine 114 times. Learned something new every single day and used the new material to prepare for the next day. Laughed and cried in joy as much as in pain just to find ourselves right here, in the evening, at this very point and know exactly: "Now, it's the whole drill all over again."

There's 1.330 miles ahead of us, another 249.711ft of altitude to ascend and another 248.049ft of altitude to descend on. Some passes, rivers and lakes, forests and infinitely vast lands – but only 57 days left. That means half the time for the same distance.

It was clear to us: Stepping it up a notch, drastically. More miles, less breaks, no zeros, faster pace and less sleep.

DAY 115   07/22/2019   MILE 1.328 - 1.346   *TRAILMAGIC*

Had a sweet long sleep and had a rough time getting into the flow. Three miles ahead of the camp we reached the road leading to Shasta and found a trail-magic-ridden hiker box. Enjoyed the pasta with sauce and veggie mix and met the Israeli and his wife. After crossing North Fork Feathers River once more we had even more trail magic behind a tree. Bananas and Gatorade fueled us for the last miles to the camp.

Adi and Ury. "Didu" and "Moment". A super chill couple and great company. Both came all the way from Israel to hike the PCT together. Since, however, the USA – or let's say certain persons – have a problem with Israelis, Adi wouldn't have the possibility to be hiking from the very beginning. She received the visa with a delay and hence joined in Shasta. Both are slim and tall, dark hair and always with a smile on their face.

The only difference is that Ury looks like the average PCT hiker while Adi looks all dapper with styled hair and patch-free clothing.

We had met Ury before already shortly ahead of KM-South and were instantly asked to take their first common picture for them. Since then we never ran into each other again. Funnily though, we met half a year later in Australia.

DAY 116   07/23/2019   MILE 1.346 - 1.370

Straight thru Lasson NP, barely and ascents but lots of downhill, straight paths. Did roughly 23.5 PCT miles but got lost in between and only noticed ¾ miles into the wrong way. Spotting a baby deer with its mother made up for the extra mile. The detour caused our feet to get wet twice for having to cross the river, but they'd dry quickly as it was rather warm today again.

DAY 117   07/24/2019   MILE 1.370 - 1.394

This morning it was f***ing cold!
We chalked off the first miles with gloves until having a break at a cave by the PCT that was shaped by lava. It was 8°C inside when we explored it a little bit and when we returned outside, the sun was at the zenith. In flaming heat we marched across lava rocks and luckily mostly on even grounds. Our sleeping place is at the "Cache 22", a water tank that's being maintained by some lovely people all to serve water to the hikers.

The area once more was rather flat and we were lucky to walk with some clouds, as there would have been no cover from any trees whatsoever! We felt like walking the African savanna while craving a cold coke so badly when we suddenly running into trail magic after a curve ... a cooling box all by itself ...

With ice-cold coke ... every drop was heaven on earth! Toward noon we reached Burney.

DAY 119   07/26/2019   MILE 1.411 - 1.413   (ALMOST ZERO IN
                                                       BURNEY)

We spent the night at the gym hall in church. Showered and had done laundry already the evening before. Today was all about groceries and organizing those 4 boxes. 3 boxes to resupply food, to Sead Valley and two stops in Oregon as well as a shake-down-box. The box office was about to close when we rolled in the shopping cart with our packages. In the evening, we did two more miles back on track.

"Hiker box", "resupply box", "bounce box", "food box". Everything revolves around logistics when you're in town. Sportsmen have entire teams to take care of them for a couple of hours or a few days – while hikers are to take care of themselves. Every single hiker organizes their very own supply – for whole five or six months.

Electrolytes, vitamins, medication, band-aids. The latter don't really matter anyway. You're either screwed or you just keep walking. Shoes, socks, possibly new underwear, gear-change, gas cartridges, sun screen and most importantly: Food.

This is a basic grocery list (one person) for a seven day hike:

- 5 packages of instant noodles (veggie)
- 2 packages of couscous (different flavors!)
- 2 packages of rice meals (mind the flavors, too!)
- 1-2 packages of mountain-house-meal
  (only sometimes available and preferably Pad Thai)
- 10x cliff bars (favorite: peanut butter and dark chocolate)
- 8x energy bars of different flavors
- 5x chocolate/cereal bars
- 1 package of cookies
- 1 package of tortilla (small sized)
- 1 glass of Nutella (small), 1 glass of peanut butter for you
- 1 bottle of avocado oil (250ml)
- 2-3 bags of chips (barbecue)
- 2 bags of sour apple win gum
- 1 bag of worms (win gum, not the protein)
- 1 bag of dried mangos
- 1 bag of mixed nuts (trail mix, including chocolate bits)
- 5 bags of liquid chocolate
- 10x electrolyte pills and 1x MIO (liquid electrolyte)
- salt

A bar for breakfast, nuts during the entire day, tortillas with Nutella and sometimes even butter, wine gum (4-6 pieces), five spoons of crushed chips and a second bar whilst on the move. A warm meal for dinner and at the beginning of the week, you can spoil yourself with some spoons of chips. To close the day it'd be a hot chocolate heating you up nicely before it's bed time.

This amounts to some 3.000 kcal; but you'll burn somewhere between 4.000 and 8.000 kcal on a daily, depending on the miles and altitude. Losing weight is guaranteed!

When you're not really equipped with some extra pounds the body could make use of, the drill will turn into an energy-draining torture. Some hikers, especially the female ones, deliberately gained some weight ahead of the trail in order to lose them in ease. Not me. I kept losing pounds every single week without being able to make it up – despite attempting to do so with the help of burgers, fries, coke, milk shakes and donuts whenever we'd be in town.

Losing fat, gaining muscles – which in turn ignite the fat storages making you pack more food. The backpack gains weight – the body loses it. A vicious circle to accompany you until you leave the trail.

The hiker boxes in town don't really help in relieving the backpack's weight. A blessing and a burden. Whatever one hiker doesn't need will be taken by the next one. Whether it's tent equipment, shampoo, books, socks, shoes, q-tips, food or even old sleeping bags. You'll find anything in hiker boxes and sometime even real treasure such as ridiculously delicious salmon that's still sealed and which we'd go crazy over up at Silver Pass.

The unconditional care for each other and the sense of community to be felt in these towns and on the trail anyway are tough to describe – if possible at all. It's a true gift to experience this.

Grabbing two cereal bars from the hiker box and then it's back in the game. Thank you, dear unknown hiker.

DAY 120   07/27/2019   MILE 1.413 - 1.441

Today, we finally managed to get up early (since the Sierra). Were on the trail at 5am and had done 10 miles by 10am :) So we chose to do some extra miles today. After a six mile ascent, we were utterly exhausted from the heat (supposedly 105°F) and lied down at a dirt road to have a nap. I woke up as I felt a horse to be passing us, but it was a young bear crawling up at us (and at our food). Our noises scared him off instantly and we sadly only took a picture of his butt. Handled our planned 27 miles without any major pain.

DAY 121   07/28/2019   MILE 1.441 - 1.467

This morning was tough on me. ... Had little energy and zero power in my legs so Finn prepared a protein shake for me and later on I had electrolytes enriched with caffeine! That really pushed me before my blister at the heel flared up again to take away my wanderlust for a couple of hours. But Finn cheered me up nicely and everything was fine after a while. A small deer paid us a visit when we had a break. The smoke we have been seeing in the distance since yesterday is still arising – hopefully not fire to block our path!

We used to play that back in school – out here, it's nature playing it with us.

Whether it's the countless wildfires in Oregon that attract massive thunderstorms or the cloudbursts in Washington. To leave the Sierra behind by no means equals a child's play coming at you.

It's been days that we've been hiking through burned down forests, black, coal-covered and dead trees. The heat coming from above isn't filtered by any green leaves. The warmth is being reflected from the darkened, burned woods. And there is a creaking of trunks grinding each other whenever there is a little breeze.

It's jumping over them, sometimes down below, crossing their side or doing a bigger detour to cross fallen down trees. We've gone to completely ignore this regular madness by now – we won't mount our tent here, though. The reaction time would be too short to dodge any of these giants.

Except for that one night when we simply couldn't keep walking. The black field wouldn't come to an end and we made an exception; with the condition to get going at the tiniest breeze.

After the fire, there is water and then there is the lightning. That counts for the game as much as for us right here. First, you feel a small drop on your arm, watch the sky and make up a major cluster of clouds hovering over the trees. Not enough to fully calculate the weather for the upcoming hours.

At a small clearing, however, we do see it – a massive thunder-storm in the far distance. Coming directly toward us.

"Shit, are we going back?"

"No idea. It might not pass our way. We might reach Fisher Lake before it hits us."

Turning around is (almost) never an option. So we crank it up and run! With every hour passing, we feel it stirring up. The air gets heavy and moister, and then we hear it. A rumbling in the distance, followed by a lightning and a thunder. Lightning and thunder moving closer before they unleash onto us in an instant. Rain, hail, lightning and thunder. It pours and stings. The fat hailstones feel like a thousand needles and the soaked up, cold skin doesn't do any good.

I scream and freeze.

"I don't like this! We have to find cover, I'm cold and the hail hurts!" – "Larissa, we can't pause now. Like how could we possibly mount a dry tent right now? That won't work! We have to keep going to stay warm!", you're yelling toward me with the intention of being louder than the rain.

Grumpy and with a frog in my throat I can't but cry. This is where the fun ends for me.

And there it is. A lightning, brighter than anything man-made and milliseconds onward the bang. I scream, a scream from deep within and my eyes flaring up in fear. Then it's you who scream, scream with might and main and pull me into your arms.

No fear in your eyes, just the shock about my scream. I'm shaking out of fear and coldness. Slowly I'm calming down, sink into your arms and acknowledge the fact that we have no choice but to keep walking.

We had a good start and enjoyed walking in the shade of the trees and dodging the heat as much as possible. Lots of ascent but also some downhill. It felt like we made the attempted 27 miles in a heartbeat until we realized it was just 4-5 miles. The blister at my heel started hurting like hell and I could barely put down the foot properly. This usually happens after an extended break, which today we had at a beautiful river. It was so beautiful ... the rushing sound of the river, the whispering wind in the trees coming down to cool off your bare skin. It's moments like these you want time to stand still! This definitely makes up for the blister!

It was great to sleep in once again. And quite necessary, as we had gone to bed only around 10:30pm. We easily pulled off the 7 miles to the Interstate 5 from where we'd quickly catch a ride to Mt. Shasta – without any breaks (peeing breaks not counted in ;-))
In Mt. Shasta we had super delicious sandwiches and salad, also got (bought) new socks, food and the like.
Back on the trail, we took a brief dive into Sacramento River as we had no chance to take a shower in town. Afterwards, we did 4 more miles.

As we were targeted by the mosquitos, we hurried to pack our stuff and ascended for 7 miles. Once on top, I didn't feel too well despite having had electrolytic caffeine ... exhausted & worn out! Finn suggested to take a nap (although we had already had a major break only an hour ago) ... thus I did and it felt soooo good! We resumed our journey to Porcupine Lake where Finn went skinny dipping. Oh and we met "Horse" again.

DAY 125   08/01/2019   MILE 1.531 - 1.561   *BEER-MAGIC*
                                               FIRST-30-MILE-DAY

Beer and a shot of tequila were great support in chalking off the last 1.2 miles of our first 30-mile-day so far. - Like they be suppressing the pain.

This morning we were capable of leaving the camp around 5:45am and hence were enjoying the first miles with a pristine sunrise. Passed numerous beautiful, crystal clear lakes and intended to do a whole 30 miles today as the terrain was all flat. 29 miles into the hike we were super exhausted and met 2 dudes by the highway 3 that invited us for beer and tequila – hence, making us fly, quite literally, for the last 1.2 miles.

DAY 126   08/02/2019   MILE 1.561 - 1.586

Lots of steep ascents and descents but we were spared from brutal heat. Saw many super cute chipmunks and a horde of cows. Unfortunately, we had to notice that we had calculated our food rather tight; so tomorrow we'll try to briefly go to Etna to pop some of those calories.
Going to bed with yet another amazing sunset!

He's Russian and slightly crazy, the first real "SoBo". Started just a month ago and over 1.000 miles done already, making him do some 30 miles every single day. These hikers try to cross the Sierra ahead of the fall in order to avoid snow fall, meaning no zeros at all. They have less time than us and are pulling through from the very first day on.

Shortly before, he had given his bicycle to a homeless guy with whom he'd once driven up the coast.

Now he's here, without a bicycle and telling us he'll have to be in Campo in no more than two months, as his visa is about to expire.

After picking up our jaws from the ground where they had fallen to, and in remembrance of our first 30-mile-day ever, we're asking whether he's gone completely mad. He starts laughing and gets some of our advice for his last 1.586 miles.

We go to bed early as 9pm is a good reminder that we're just past "hiker midnight".

DAY 127   08/03/2019   MILE 1.586 - 1.600

This night we had another hiker around and found out that he truly was the very first "SoBo"-hiker. We passed all those stunning lakes without bigger breaks and were attracted by the so-called "town-gravity". Arrived in Etna noonish and had a delicious burger at Dotty's. We mounted our tent in the backyard of a trail angel couple and participated in the block party that took place that night.

DAY 128   08/04/2019   MILE 1.600 - 1.614

After we had breakfast and Finn enjoyed the best shake ever (apple-pie-milkshake) we were back on the PCT at noon. Again, no extended breaks and settled down at Fisher Lake already at 6:30pm. Many salamanders in that water.

Finally, the time has come to tell about to wonderful persons and our first encounter at a small stream at mile 1.610. "Flash" and "Raider", the first two people to become close friends a few weeks later.

But for now, back to that very first encounter that surely already tells about their characteristics.

With our stomachs bloated, with little motivation equipped and with our thoughts already at today's campground – that's how we arrived. The first glance at the unexpected spring, that's ever so nicely and freshly splashing its way down. This sight was an immediate excuse to have a break right here. The second glance toward those two fellas that, too, were having a break down there.

"Holy moly, haven't you don't enough sport today?", I'm smiling toward one of them, who was amidst of doing really fast pushups.

"We need to keep up our upper body muscle", the other one smirks back and turns serious as he monitors the wound down his ankle.

We look at each other and conclude the same thought: "Those two sure have a screw loose!".

Nevertheless, we do engage in a conversation and find out they already did 30 miles today and have another 10 coming at them. That wound thing at his ankle apparently has been going on for a while but the lack of time kept them from seeing a doctor. Apparently, he has done the AT – Appalachian Trial – before, with a broken leg, what had been way more painful.

"Raider" (Philip) is in his 50s, a former US marine and spares no time for boring stuff. His figure resembles a 30-year old bodybuilder and his mentality that one of a hyper little boy that can't wait to dive into the next adventure. He's always on the lookout for the next experimental excursion, and the grey, short-shaved soldier is always available with his life experience whenever you need him.

He stayed with "Flash" with a major sense of responsibility.

"Flash" (Cory), doesn't look less of a bodybuilder but has quite the opposite visuals and character of "Raider". Calm, planned out and equipped with some of his Japanese mother's traits. While "Raider" would jump ten steps at once, "Flash" would rather take a step back to fully evaluate the situation.

Both, however, sport massive care for each other and have highest priority to watch out for one another – regardless of the when- & whereabouts. A trait of integrity you won't find in many people these days.

"Flash", too, served his country. They are deeply connected through their past career – him, being a Navy-Seal in the past perfectly harmonizes with "Raider". They only met at the PCT but since then have become inseparable.

They'd be hiking until 3pm and then would wait for each other, no matter how long, no matter where and during which weather conditions and no matter how fit you'd still be. That is a promise and if the other wouldn't show up, they'd be out there searching.

Over the coming days and weeks we kept running into them. Would meet them whenever they'd pass us yet another time. In Island horses you'd call their pace tölt which equals something between fast hiking and actual running. Always with a severe expression and with focus on their target they hiked pass us quickly, disappearing in the bushes and leaving nothing to see but shaking leaves. And we'd be surprised every time they'd pass us from behind once more.

At this point I'd like to mention how thankful we are to have met these two fellas down at the small creek as they were doing their training.

DAY 129   08/05/2019   MILE 1.614 - 1.644

Another 30 Mile Day done!
The first 20 miles were a constant up and down, quite steep, which we aren't used to down at the PCT ... no wonder the mood wasn't the best ;-)
But that's alright, the last 10 miles were just downward. We witnessed particularly many colorful butterflies at the springs today, some deer and a stag.

DAY 130   08/06/2019   MILE 1.644 - 1.662

Finally slept in ... until 6am ... then walked off the 12 miles all the way to Seiad Valley at a constant pace for five hours straight. Picked some blackberries on our way and we met "Funk" some 5 miles ahead of town to accompany us for the remaining hike. He'd already done 22 miles by then. Had delicious food at Seiad Café, milkshakes, coke & Gatorade, writing post cards, took a shower and arranged food packages. Chilled some time before doing another 6 miles at some chilly 97°F while ascending a really steep mountain. We're sleeping at the ridge ... Oregon, here we come! ... another 29.5 miles ...

DAY 131   08/07/2019   MILE 1.662 - 1.692   *TRAILMAGIC*
                                                    OREGON BABY

This morning we had some small trail magic by two former 2019-hikers. Shortly afterwards, Finn felt dizzy as we were ascending and needed some sugar. Well, he currently carries both our food. At some point it got a little cloudy and eased

the final miles to Oregon. Around 7:30pm we made it ...
byebye California and hello Oregon.
I left one dreadlock back in California.

Oregon Baby

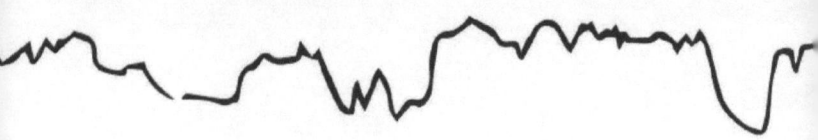

We go for the 14-day-challenge

A new state, a new challenge. The last four months made us fit, we lost weight and built muscle, gained experience and crushed doubts. For 2.700km along the coast of California we busted through desert and snow, battled rivers and mountains, learned what it means to be free, what it means to be bound and the promise to be bound to each other and watch out for. Here we are, in front of a small wooden board telling us we're finally entering the second out of three states.

We had been picturing this moment for so long, were so excited to reach it, so happy to be chalking of an entire state, advancing, discovering something new.

Man is a weird creature that has tough times advancing without a task. To focus on a task instead of just living as it comes. Our actions and deeds have altered drastically with evolutionary developments. The goal to merely survive barely exists and hence we learned to put down new, individual goals. That might be more or less goals, depending on the person. But the sum of it shapes our existence and fuels us.

We're restlessly walking 40 or 50 kilometers a day, cross passes and hop over wild rivers with a cold mouth. We're proving to ourselves the capability of going above and beyond every single evening. We're restless because our target lies upon one goal – a goal set by ourselves, and that would be Oregon ... for now.

Here we are now, the path is sandy and the bushes green. Nature remains the same, green doesn't turn red, sand doesn't turn rocky – everything stays the same.

Purely the small wooden board lets us quietly know to have achieved the first part. No orchestral reception, no trumpets, no fireworks, no red carpet, no people or let alone cheering masses to receive us. Just you and I, standing there, after a 30-mile-day, all sweaty, calm, equilibrated and ever so happy. A kiss on the mouth and a quick picture in front of the board and the entry into the ready trail register conclude the whole deal officially.

We crawl up utterly tired to the closest spot to mount the tents for the night. There is daylight left and we are gladly cleaning our feet to celebrate the milestone. Despite socks and shoes, there is no single patch that's not covered in dust, dirt and sand. From the tip of ours toes all the way to the shirts the sand covers our bodies like a thin layer of patina. The sand has a great time getting caught up in your leg hair. Which is why you prefer sleeping with long pants as to avoid spending time to clean up the dirt.

As of tomorrow, shit is about to get real. The challenge awaits us and we are ready to rule. We are headed into the fortnight-challenge with "clean" legs and feet. 14 days to master 455 miles, equaling a staggering 32.5 miles a day without a single zero-day, obviously.

52 kilometers a day result in a straight 10-hour hike at a pace

of 5-6 km/h – without any breaks.

Some people do their 9-5 while we are doing the 7-5 hiking style, all while including sports, being out in nature, watching fauna and doing adventures.

However, it is with a good reason we are taking on this challenge. Out of the three states, Oregon is the flattest one – it isn't actually flat, though. But the usual 13.000ft of daily difference in altitude now shrink down to some 7.000ft. We want to take advantage of that in order not to get in trouble as we reach Washington. In order to board our planes back home September 17.

We had already packed for that in Burney and sent them to Oregon. They're awaiting us in Mazama Village and Big Bear Youth Camp. The plan is to run until we're completely done and to spend little time in those places, rendering us icecold heroes.

The Bridge of Gods is our goal for the 21st of August, leading us to our third and final state, Washington. That'll leave us 24 days to end the PCT by September 14 and hitch hike to Seattle all relaxed, where our plane to Hamburg will depart from. And most importantly: It'll give us a night at a luxury hotel comforting us with a bath tub.

With this goal in mind we dive into the challenge highly motivated – into another day on the PCT.

DAY 132   08/08/2019   MILE 1.692 - 1.724

Despite a troublesome night we got up pretty easily and found ourselves on the trail at 5:30am with lamps on our head. We immediately had a mind-blowing view in the early morning! The valley lay in front of us with clouds shaping up to an ocean, where single mountain peaks would pierce through, resembling islands in the sea of clouds. At 10am we had already mastered 11.9 miles, but tiredness came through at the next climb. Almost fell asleep during the walk so we did go for a lunch break with a nap. Finn wasn't able to sleep but I felt great afterwards. Did our first 32.5 miles by 8:30pm.

DAY 133   08/09/2019   MILE 1.724 - 1.750 (AN ENTRY BY FINN)

Took off on time at 5:20am and wanted to seize the day but the last days' exhaustion stuck with us already during the first 10 miles. To regain energy, Finn hitch hiked to Green Springs Inn and got us lunch, drinks and an avocado. Larissa took the time to nap. Within one hour and the funniest hitch (parrot) we went on to Howard Prairie Lake where we enjoyed a hot shower and an early night.

"Well sweetie, slept well? You won't believe what kind of dude just gave me a ride!", you're laughing as you present the food your brought us.

"Yea, I heard you guys coming. Dude, what kind of music was that?", am I wondering.

"That was the sickest hitch ever."

Your experience can't wipe off the smile off your face as you tell the story.

"So, first I was like at the hotel where I had some nice, freshly drawn beer. Freakin' good, I had two."

You smirk as you keep telling.

"They guys over there were super kind and the host made me this delicious sandwich as I told him what we are doing out here. Oh, and the family that brought me here – they weren't planning on driving here, but they said no big deal to detour me up here. It's crazy how friendly people are around here! Oh, and sadly they were out of apples but I got you an avocado. Thought you might like it."

You're winking and getting the avocado out the paper bag.

"Oh god, I love you. Thank you, I totally want this right now!"

I'm opening the avocado right away and spoon it whilst carefully listening to you.

"Well, and then I had to come back. And in came the most worn out dude ever. The host told him to take me back up the trail head. His car's hood was completely gone and the rest looked like total trash, too. My pants are totally wet, no idea what was on that seat."

You're flashing your butt and laughing as I feel your wet pants. I'm disgusted and smell my hand but can't define the liquid.

Fully amused and with my mouth packed am I answering: "Good thing we can take a shower in a few days."

"So nasty. But the best part was this tramp had a fuckin parrot."

"What? Like a real parrot? No way!"

"For real, a living parrot that was seated on top of his steering wheel and would move in curves."

I'm shaking my head, laugh and can't believe that once again you experienced awesome shit like this.

"And one time, the parrot sat on his arm that was half outside the window and almost got blown away by the wind. All so fuckin weird, let alone the music."

"Yeah, I heard that as you arrived. Woke me up actually."

"So what's up with you?", are you asking as you finish up your story.

"Well, so I slept and then "Blue Suite Man" came up thinking I was dead. No idea. That guy is weird. He's walking ahead of us now. Want a sip of coke?"

"Blue Suite Man", a man in a blue overall, tall, skinny and might as well be employed as a janitor in Scrubs. Likes to carry his water bag by hand just because he can. Has no hiking sticks and the suit covering his long sleeves is a little too short at the legs, well revealing his worn out, simple sneakers. A big hat and a grumpy face expression as he loves condescend to his fellow hikers. He's already done the AT – also in a blue overall. It's been a few days now that we've been passing each other. Odd bird.

DAY 134   08/10/2019   MILE 1.750 - 1.773

The thunderstorm woke us up a couple of times and the soothing rain helped us fall back asleep. Kept re-programming the alarm all the way to 7:00am when rain had finally come to a hold.

Started off with blue skies until noon, when rain came back down. When having a peeing break, a baby chipmunk fell out of a tree straight in front of us. We carefully shoved it off the trail with our sticks. Possibly it'll recover soon. When it rained and hailed once more, heavy thunderstorm, too, kicked in. For the last 9 miles to reach Fisher Lake Resort, we basically ran with the goal of getting a hot shower after 4 hours of getting soaked by the rain.

DAY 135   08/11/2019   MILE 1.773 - 1.801

Took off at Fisher Lake Camp Ground at 8am and had to do 1.3 miles before being back at the PCT. Thankfully, it was rather plain today so we advanced well. We dried our stuff during lunch break and later on a chipmunk baby crossed our path ... incredibly cute!
Finn is quite worn out today ... feet, heels, legs, head altogether!

DAY 136   08/12/2019   MILE 1.801 - 1.823   *MAZAMA VILLAGE*

We didn't take off our pajamas when we left because it was darn cold. With pee on my glove and crap on my finger we made it in under 8 hours all the way to Mazama Village, chalking off 20 miles. Resupply-box (turned out just fine!), did laundry and ate before hiking some more at 7:30pm. "Sunshine" & Tyler are hot on our trail.

DAY 137   08/13/2019   MILE 1.823 - 1.856

Since the PCT is closed for the upcoming 16 miles (due to high occurrence of mountain lions crossing caused by wildfires) , we're having to walk Crater Lake Rim Trail, being shorter by 5 miles leaving us do "only" 28 miles instead of 33 ;-) Anyhow, this detour was totally worth it as we had an amazing view along the entire Rim Trail over Crater Lake (deepest lake in the US). Walked the entire time with Tom "Polka Dots" and chatted a lot.

"Polka Dots" also known as Tom is from Hamburg and does the first 10 miles of the day in barefoot-shoes. They resemble socks and leave a small but neat polka dot pattern in the ground. Him, too, is tall, skinny and has grown a respectable beard over time. He is a trained physiotherapist and highly educated in alimentation and sports, passing on his knowledge on those topics to us as we move. Business ideas as well as possible future collaborations are discussed. You and I as mushroom-guides while he provides lectures on sports. We're not having the floor as much though, as Tom won't stop once he is on fire. Making miles appear short which is also because we'd do some jogging just for fun. A workout within a workout one could say.

Exactly two months later, 13 October, we'd do Lübeck Marathon altogether in record times.

DAY 138   08/14/2019   MILE 1.856 - 1.885

Went to bed in a wet tent and woke up in a dry one ... dream come true! Hiked again with Tom and had time fly by. Finn, however, did have serious troubles with his Achilles tendon that he fought off with a smaller ibu (400) and reduced weight (I took the food bag) – it worked not too bad. Not as many views up in Oregon like in California – if you have a view, it's all trees! To round off the day, Finn got stung by a wasp. Nevertheless, we almost did 30 miles.

"So do you believe in life after death?", a voice slicing the silence out of a sudden.

Tom, who was walking behind me, had been silent for a while before popping this question.

Since you're subject to tremendous pain, you don't feel like answering and I jump in: "Don't know, hard to imagine a complete void after life. Like this void is so tough to imagine, right?"

"I agree", Tom turns pensive.

"Why are you asking?"

"Well, already during preparation phase for the PCT I found myself caught up in thoughts on that. It's not far-fetched to leave your life on the trail". Tom speaks as if he was discussing the weather.

"Yeah that's true", I'm responding.

"Before I left, I'd gather all my passwords and documents to leave them with my girlfriend in case anything happened. Kind of a weird sensation to prepare for that."

"Crazy, we didn't plan that far ahead. Of course we organized and put down some stuff and left it accessible. Also Finn's mother knows where to find stuff, but that's more like university stuff."

I'm diving contemplatively into the topic.

"Well you guys are walking as two, for something to happen to the both of you is a rather rare possibility. But you never know! I've been thinking I should be setting up my will."

I freeze in a perplexed fashion, gather my thoughts before I get going again as Tom almost runs into me.

"Actually you're right. Surely, as a youngster you don't really think about it but one really can die leaving everyone else in the dark. Weird, I've never thought about that. I even thought it was odd to discuss this matter with my mother very recently. That, however, concerned my grandpa who now finally puts down a patient's provision."

"Anyway, I'll write my will as soon as I get home. Doesn't have to include a lot and I have nothing to bequeath either way." Tom laughs but I'm sensing the topic's importance in his voice. I'm contemplating the concept of dying. Being alive and from one moment to another simply fading away. And suddenly I realize I've actually had these thoughts numerous times. You and I – in unity ever so happy that it feels like a dream. In the past years, I'd frequently find myself unable to fully grasp the luck I was having with you. To be walking on the same right path with you for all those years. My happiness was too big as if this could go on forever. My happiness was too beautiful to not be stopped out at some point.

By some divine forces I'd always somehow sense the fact that we'd eventually encounter this very obstacle. If anyone was capable of handling tough times, it would be us. I somehow knew, there would be something at some point but it wouldn't matter – we had each other. I've got you and you've got me – and whatever we'd be facing we'd tackle off together.

I somewhat thought I'd develop a disease from within and I'd die soon. I don't know what gave me the idea that my utter luck could not be the ultimate sensation for me to feel, and it actually turned me very pensive. I'm painting a horrible picture. Not for me, but for you. To not think about leaving you with unimaginable pain, seeing you hurt badly. I wouldn't care about myself as I'd be without feelings anyway – or would I not?! Well, you don't really know which makes the whole deal so fascinating. Nobody can tell you what it's like on the other side. To no longer roam the Earth in the body you're given but follow the soul to new endeavors.

Back at the PCT, step by step and leaving behind the last miles as if it were a blackout. I'm asking Tom: "So what do you put down in a will?"

"Well, that there's gonna be a big party, that's for sure!"

Tom cracks up and so do I.

"Oh for sure. And I want nobody, really nobody to show up in black clothes! They shall be colorful and cheer for my life with music and singing!", I'm adding to your thoughts.

"And you're supposed to state your preference as to be put into the ground or want to be burned", "Polka Dots" explains.

"God, that's like the toughest thing to imagine! You're cramped into a coffin in the earth, you're dead and yet parts of you are still there, having people step on you for 100 years. Ideally I'd dissolve with my body into air. Simply vanish and be no longer.", I'm saying before you're telling us: "I want to be cremated and my ashes shall be spread across the whole planet."

I'm laughing and ask with a smirk: "So who'll be the lucky one to do that?"

"Well, that would be you!"

You halt, turn around to me and wink at me.

"Funny, so I'll do that when I'm like a hundred years old or what?!"

"Exactly..."

The three of us start laughing.

Still mosquitos from last night around which sped up the packing part!

Had our second break at a beautiful creek and then it's 10 miles straight to Shelter Cove for burgers and coke. We met Zack again and then walked for another 8 miles till we reached a pretty neat hut directly at the PCT ... was a little scary though. :-)

DAY 140   08/16/2019   MILE 1.914 - 1.943   *1. DREAD OUT*
                                                   2ND WASP STING FOR FINN

We woke up in the hut where it was colder than expected and got going at 8am. Today, just like yesterday, we passed endless lakes and would spend every break by the shore of a beautiful lake. Were a little down around noon but then kicked 11 miles in 2 hours. Then we had dinner and another 1.8 miles up to Horse Shoe Lake.

DAY 141   08/17/2019   MILE 1.943 - 1.975

The day started with "smoke on the water", we managed 10 by 10 and had a whole 15.5 miles by noon. We were highly motivated and were rushing at like 4 miles an hour for half an hour – equaling a jog. Had dinner at Obsidian Fall! ... One of the most stunning places at the PCT. Sleeping next to rocks made of lava.

"Hey sweetie, so what's up?", my dad asks me.

He looks deep into my eyes while I'm sitting with torn hiking clothes and all dirty on the sofa at my parents' in Kremperheide.

"I'm worn out and tired and missing you guys. Where is mom?"

"She's getting some food for you. You seem to be really hungry, how much weight have you lost?"

"Like a lot but that doesn't matter. I'm just really missing you. When is mom coming back? I'll have to get going shortly. Alarm clock is about to ring and then I'm gone."

"There she is."

"Hey Muschel, some food for you here."

"Thanks mom, but I gotta get going. So sorry, I wish I could stay longer!"

My parents' faces fade into foggy smoke, my face is wet. I wake up in tears, my heart hurts and I want to go home.

"Everything fine darling?", you're asking after seeing another tear run down my cheek.

"I've just had a dream with mom and dad and at the same time I knew I was here and couldn't stay with them. That felt so real, absolutely crazy. I'm missing them, I can't do it anymore, Finni ..."

I'm bursting into tears and lie down onto your chest.

You're putting your arms around me with love and caress me.

"We'll give them a call in the next town and you'll be with them in just a month. Come here."

I'm feeling your energy run through me, let myself sink into your arms and enjoy this moment. Time stands still and for this moment it's certain: Everything will be fine because you are with me.

Through Mordor and all the way to Mount Doom ... or something like that! Walked through lava rocks almost the entire day and luckily didn't trip once. Arrived at Big Lake Youth Camp around noon, took a shower, did laundry and got our food package. Also got the lost bag with the electric stuff that one girl had sent to us. ... *trail magic* ... then it's another 7 miles.

DAY 143   08/19/2019   MILE 2.002 - 2.031

This morning, Tom woke us up at 5:30am telling us he has a flight for September 22 which is why (also because he has diarrhea) he is driving back to Sisters ... Hence, it's just the two of us again before "Blue Suite Man" got to us.
Walked a lot through burned down woods and uphill which

made us advance not as well. Also some home sickness and temporary aversion (once again) hit. Nevertheless, we did 28.5 mikes.

Home Sickness, Missing, Heartache, Yearning

The desire for a human without whom life seems harder.

We've learned a lot and experienced stories on our paths thus far enabling us to deal with physical pain, breathing it away or simply accepting it and keep going. But what's with the pain inside of us, the pain of our souls. To ignore it, swallow it and simply march on works until a certain point – but sooner or later it'll hit you like a cannon ball.

You'd think out here in nature it'll be easier to deal with home sickness or the feeling of yearning as we are surrounding by pure beauty. The focus has shifted through all the pristine views and the daily hikes massively distract. Certainly, that's true to an extent. But the other end features a mental and physical toll arching across your own growth and the fight against the individually set limits. To carry an emotional chaos within surpasses any human nature and shapes up to daily, hourly or minutely breakdowns. Each of those requires another growth from within and lets you gain enormous psychological strength.

I can't tell whether Tom suffers from heartache but surely I feel he is missing his girlfriend and little son.

He records audio messages for them on a daily basis, covering his experiences and talking about how many rivers he had to cross again. Talks about how beautiful it is out here and how sad he is not to have them with him. Their relationship has reached a point where she is forced to arrange herself with the situation and the long distance across half the globe. Bearing the fear not knowing whether your boyfriend will return safe and sound. Waiting back home all powerless until the loved person will return – and Tom on the other side missing an entire half a year of development of his son.

There's always a bundle of several messages to be sent the next time there is a chance – as well as downloading the answers to the previous messages. The WIFI at times seems a leftover from the Stone Age making its use a real drag. Due to the lack of time people listen to the voice messages somewhere out in nature, where again there is no possibility of sending a response but notes are taken as to respond the next time possible. So much for digital love letters.

DAY 144   08/20/2019   MILE 2.031 - 2.060

First of all, it's ascending for 5.5 miles of which the last 2 were unusually steep ... but the view up there once again was tremendous ... at Mt. Jefferson (and its glacies) and Mt. Hood.
Previously, we had crossed a fairytale-like meadow and also the view from the "other" side of the ascent was marvelous. From there on, it was almost entirely downhill. Had some cooling drinks at Olallie Lake and couscous with ramen. It all left my body very quickly. Apparently you can walk off stomach issues though. 15 miles in I'm feeling a lot better.

"Finn, I think I need a bathroom quickly", I'm saying and my face sports uneasiness.

"We've just taken off. Why didn't you go back at the camping spot?"

"I hadn't had to yet. Let's find a neat spot real quick. I hardly dare to let one rip by now."

You crack up really loud and mock me: "There is no KFC close by."

"That's not funny and I dare you tell this to anyone else."

With half a smirk and all pain on my face I keep walking. No place to go as far as the eye can see and the stomach noises are increasing. As I launch the careful attempt to release some gas, I notice something went wrong terribly.

"Finn, please don't laugh. I think I just messed up badly."

You freeze, turn around and look me in the eyes whilst trying so hard not to burst into laughter. Then I start laughing and you join in.

"Yeah well, I think it looks great back there!"

I walk behind you like a kid with a shit-loaded diaper.

A few more steps, off the backpack, out the "poop kit" and quickly into the next bushes.

Digging the hole comes in really tough as your body is already prepared to let loose while you squat down, all ready to drop it with those impatient intestines.

Pants down and go. I'm so grateful to finally give in the roaring noises when witnessing the utter mess in my underwear.

"Fiiiihiiiiin?", I'm screaming from the makeshift toilet in the bushes.

"Yes! Everything alright?", you're shouting back.

"More or less, I need new underwear! Could you get me some from my backpack? But don't come here!"

I do hear you smirking in spite of the distance and fully grant you the fun moment full of schadenfreude and smirk about myself.

All clean – toilet paper sealed in the Ziploc, the hole covered with earth and I return half naked with dirty underwear in my hands.

"Anybody here?", I'm asking you with the voice down.

"Like who? The shitsie-monster?", you're laughing.

"Not funny! No, like other hikers. I have to change fast."

"Oh man, you're really cute, did you know?!"

You're winking as you give me a kiss on the forehead.

DAY 145   08/21/2019   MILE 2.060 - 2.095

Biggest day so far (and probably of the entire hike), 35 miles. Before noon had already conquered 15 miles and then drizzling rain kicked in. Sometimes more sometimes less. We couldn't really tell as the forest was densely grown. The feet were hurting tremendously today (blisters) but after a while you'd stop feeling anything and then suddenly I got stung by something. I saw the mark on my skin but no animal to be found. Fair enough, keep hiking.

Finally reached the water after 35 miles when it was almost entirely dark already and out of a sudden it rained cats and dogs amidst mounting the tents.

I entered the tent somewhat dry but Finn was all wet. Still naked and in the middle of changing clothes another hiker stopped by asking for refuge in our tent as he only had a tarp which turned out to be all wet by now. While we had been cooking and eating we did grant him that refuge and also prepared a warm Nalgene for him ... his sleeping bag wasn't as wet. Hopefully the sun will be out tomorrow.

DAY 146   08/22/2019   MILE 2.095 - 2.119

Woke up and the rain was gone. Two miles in the hike at the Timberline Lodge we dried our stuff and had delicious buffet. Got delayed leaving that place for having exchanged some words with mom and dad, but eventually did another 22 miles in the afternoon.

DAY 147   08/23/2019   MILE 2.119 - 2.147   CASCADE LOCKS
                                              BRIDGE OF THE GODS

Alarm clock at 3:30am ... 4:30am putting on the backpack ... 4:31am Larissa smashes her shinbone :(... 4:35am back on trail.

As we marched toward the Bridge of The Gods during sunrise, I was completely done at times! No more energy reserves (scale shows 46.5kg/102.5lbs) and my body and mind really didn't want to move on. But Finn flashes great skills of motivation.

We managed to reached Cascade Locks one hour prior to the post office closing and retrieved 4 packages, resupplying for WA and sent off three food packages and the bounce box. Freshly showered and stomachs full are we now waiting for laundry before it's off to bed – finally!

Huckleberry Country

The final state - Washington

"Finn? Are you picking those berries again?"

"No!"

I stand still, turn around and look in your face. I'm dying of laughter. Your cheeks are fully blown like a hamster's and your lips and hands blueberry-purple. Really useless to deny. With a big smile you're opening up to flash the huckleberry in your mouth.

"Damn Finni, you don't even know whether those are edible."

"Of course! That's what the guy said the other day and I totally remembered what they look like."

Eyebrows raised and shaking my head – I turn around and walk on.

"Hey by the way I knew you'd turn around!", you're mocking me.

"Yeah, right.", I'm responding in irony but can't resist to smile fully in love as I keep my eyes on the track.

In silence we cross all those countless bushes. Some minutes later I freeze again and directly turn around to you. You're sporting a massive smile but this time no huckleberries in your mouth.

"I knew you'd turn around again", are you telling me with an even bigger smile.

I look into your eyes in love, move a step closer and give you a long sweet kiss on your mouth.

We're silent for a few seconds, look at each other and completely enjoy the moment.

Then I turn around again and keep walking with a tingle in my stomach.

"Uhm, Larry?"

"Yes!"

"I knew you would kiss me."

"Is that so? I also knew that you know that I was about to do that."

We walk on without any further words but we're knowing exactly what the other was thinking.

455 miles in 16 days. We didn't achieve the 14-day-challenge and yet we did do our daily 45-50km. When you're doing so many kilometers, your thoughts spin in circles and you seem to go nuts.

You're walking for hours and there is absolutely nothing around you but magical nature. You're thinking nothing and everything. Sometimes the same thing twice. Catchy songs in your head almost driving you insane. Songs that never seem to leave you and that've been haunting you for three days. You're trying to forget them and start humming them as you give up – driving your hiking partner crazy. Now he's haunted with it again – with that catchy tune.

Often times you'd enrich my mornings with that. We wake up, pack our stuff and then you go for it. You're humming, singing and laughing.

"No, stop it.", I'm saying to you, "please, Finni", am I begging you laughing and poke you ... it's too late. Three hours into the trail and I'm still humming.

Sometimes it's merely your last words popping up in my head every now and then.

"So when would be the next creek?" ... "next creek, next creek, the next creek, creek, creek again! What? God, what are you thinking about?!"

My head is all chaos and I didn't notice miles into the hike what actually was going on in my head – which was a complete void. Then it's all happiness whenever the other one starts a conversation and we enjoy to keep it up. That's the origin of our van – a van of our dreams. It's supposed to have five sleeping spots because at some point there will be three kids at least – we agreed on that one.

"And Birger can always pick them up from kindergarten", you're saying.

"Yes, that would be cool, but let's hope he won't forget them at the construction sites ...", I'm replying with a smile and we start laughing.

Possibly two sleeping spots will do in the beginning, plus most definitely a tent on the roof! There even was a place for the toolbox. The one you had gotten us in Australia and we had driven around through the outback on our three cars for two years and eventually had sent to Germany for lots of money. In our minds, we're arranging all our camping gear. A flower-bed by the window and a multi-functional working space to be folded up, turning into a "bath". Stash room above the driver's cabin or possibly a nice sleeping area? And a white kitchen front.

"No, no way that's gonna be white", are you disagreeing. "More like blue or orange!"

The ice axes we're still needing here would later on be turned into handles and the bear canister will be equipped with rubber bands serving as a water bag for our upcoming kayak trip. Once across the Baltic Sea up to Langeland.

The highlight is supposed to be an old trunk. Some bigger holes are to serve as small stashing cubicles. Able to be rotated as it is mounted with pins on top and at the bottom. Every hole is to be painted in a different color.

"We'll be saying 'the keys are in the blue box', coming in like so handy!", I'm explaining to you as you smirk.

A working space for me to be drawing on our journeys is also included in the plan – and portholes for windows.

"And definitely an open way to the driver's cabin, in case there is one!", are you saying. But we haven't agreed on a model yet. An old UPS-bus or something smaller perhaps. An old US school bus or better a Landcruiser with a mountable top?!

Prior to the trip, I had promised to get a Landcruiser off our first money after the studies. One of the older models that are still like a square.

There is no end in sight when browsing our future. At each our adventures we would be planning the next one already. Were excited for what was next and were always eager to dive into life.

"When I'm old, I want to be sitting in my rocking chair at the porch down in Australia or New Zealand, watching my land

and be blazing one up.", is what you had announced after our 2.5 year journey.

Until then, it'll be pulling through and take up any chance you'll ever get. Your motto: "Just do it!"

You were a role model for others so many times. You inspired them to walk the talk instead of just blabbering around.

No matter what came to your mind you'd go do it. I can't say you always finished what you started but that's only because you already had the next thing in mind and couldn't wait to get going.

That's how our imaginative van changes on a daily basis. We're constantly coming up with new and different ideas. Trash old ones and dig them up again a few days later to start from scratch. Too many images in mind as if it was possible to squeeze them into one van. But one thing is certain, it'll be unique and it'll be ours. The life space we are creating to feel home in, to travel in and to live in as if there was no tomorrow. Equipping it with ideas as if we were to live for centuries to come. We're simply living life and if it was to end tomorrow we'll have made the best of it.

We were aware of the danger we might be encountering on the PCT. We also knew that some hikers left their lives out in nature without returning. We also were prepared for something to happen to us and yet went our way. Haven't regretted a single day and enjoyed this life where the line between life and death is so utterly fine.

It feels weird to be putting down these lines right now. Not for me, because I'm still living this sensation. The freedom and the life power you have where you are to mobilize all your physical and psychic forces in order to advance over the pass after hours. You have to fight to advance like that and you don't have the possibility to give up. Nobody tells you: "That's enough, you just need 50% in order to succeed". No, you are to give 100% at all times. And sometimes more, as to stay focused enough to yet again cross that one river and keep marching for another 10 miles.

No, I understand, can fully related when anyone tells me: "I'll do it even if I die."

But writing it down and knowing that the readers have lost their son out there is damn tough. To be telling them how happy you were out here and attempting to ease their pain slightly. Because you truly did find the sensation of freedom out here, what you had been looking for ever since you were free around your mother's safety as a youngster. You – us, we found this feeling out there and loved it. A sensation that no words do sufficient justice to describe. A sensation that once it gets a hold of you won't ever let go. Not even when you leave the trail, are happy, enjoy a shower again, get served real dinner, put on fresh clothes and have a roof above your head – you still know: You want to be back!

DAY 148   08/24/2019   MILE 2.147 - 2.160
1ST DAY WASHINGTON   *BEST TRAILMAGIC EVER!*

The best trail magic on the trail (so far) ... "Raider" and "Flash", and "Flash's" family, respectively, presented incredible trail magic directly at the Bridge of The Gods. Not only did they prepare tons of food but they also provided masses of resupplying stuff like food, laundry stuff and first aid tools ... really rad!

That's why we only crossed the bridge to Washington around 1pm. Quite the nice feel, entering the final state of three! The last 505 miles.

A massive ascent expected us that we mastered with Melli "Flowers" from Berlin. Put down the tent fairly early around 7pm for a change.

"Flowers from Berlin" is sufficient and literal explanation for her character. A true Berlin native – and, since I haven't met too many people from Berlin, fitting straight my imagination of what I believe this would be like. But this certainly would not suffice to describe her very special kind.

The first thing you'd think of whenever she shows up as fast as a rabbit is: "Oh boy, that's a lot of pink." The second thing is: "Hell, she sure smokes a lot!"

However, the judgment of her cigarette consumption might be distorted as really not too many people in the US seem to be smoking, even less so on the trail. Whenever you see someone smoke it is almost as exciting as witnessing a bear pop up.

So what else is she up to? A professional fast-walker, fast-talker whilst lighting up a cigarette. She's somewhat like a bumblebee where it makes no physical and aeronautical sense to be flying in the first place but it's still managing to do so. I like bumblebees.

DAY 149   08/25/2019   MILE 2.160 - 2.188

Alarm clock rings at 6am but we didn't get up until 30-45 minutes later. It was super foggy and we had to descend all that altitude first before crossing the next bigger hill.

Welcome to Washington. ;-)

We thrived on the motivation of being so close to our goal, making it quite easy to pass all those ascents ... and after each ascent, it's usually downwards.

DAY 150   08/26/2019   MILE 2.188 - 2.209   *TRAILMAGIC*
                                                  FINAL DIARY ENTRY

Trail-magic-day! We reached the campground with "Flowers" after 11 miles and were received with trail magic. We sat there from 11am until 4pm, were chatting with fellow arriving hikers and had some food.

No more pressure to chalk of miles like the pressure we had back in Oregon, so nice!

Then it was another 10.5 miles to Bear Lake with "Flash" and "Rider" who obviously caught up with us by now.

"...Man, do you even know whatever life is good for?

What regularity means for you

whenever destiny screws you over?

And you forget to pick up your lunch box in the morning.

But you won't notice until arriving at your 9-5.

It ain't as easy as y'all think my man.

It's a daily hustle and it's gonna break your back..."

- Translation from the song "Nordisch by Nature" by Fettes Brot -

Sometimes life unfolds entirely unsolicited ways before us. Sometimes it's the lunch box as nicely put by Fettes Brot, sometimes it's something else. Some people say they can anticipate, feel, whatever is forthcoming. Possibly, all of us are capable of doing so – we just lack the tools to notice it.

After every stretch in the Sierra, after busting endless ups and downs, crossing all those dangerous passes and conquering hazardous rivers I told mom: "Don't you worry, we're past the critical part right now!" And every time she'd answer: "You didn't even tell me it was going to be this tough." No mom, I didn't because I didn't want you to worry already ahead of it, knowing we'd face the most dangerous part. No, I didn't want to do so because it wouldn't do any good anyway.

But now, that we really did leave the most dangerous part behind us I'm relieved to actually tell you without saving you with a lie: "Mom, everything will be fine, we'll be home in three weeks and the remaining path is "just" hiking. No snowy passes, no big rivers and no lifeless deserts."

We were relaxed, that's true. Nothing could happen to us, it'll just be walking off the remaining miles, and in our minds we already were lying in our hotel room, celebrating the conquest of this long hike.

Sometimes I wish, we had forgotten our lunch boxes at the kitchen table, missed the plane and driven our lives to other horizons.

But that's not how it works. We can't escape our destiny or however you'd like to call it.

I've put down this last diary entry on the last page of my diary and was angry now having to write the rest on lose papers – not remotely considering, that this is not going to happen anyhow.

Last Two Days

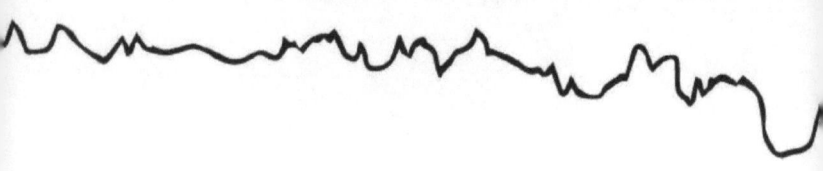

Woke up to the smell of cigarettes. Instantly felt taken back to Langeland, where often times I'd wake up to my mother's cigarette smoke in the mornings. Which is how I'd always know, someone is awake already – it felt nice.

And so it's back, the homesickness.

Not in Langeland, but at this dirt road (service rd. 68) we find ourselves on with those other hikers that, however, just walk parts of the PCT. Germans, Swiss and an American.

Like always, to the surprise of "Flowers", we have our stuff packed in our tents already and are ready to get going. "Of course", I'm saying and go around the corner to pee. Fueled by a protein bar it'll be a four-mile ascent and once we're on top, we're rewarded with a miraculous view across the mountains of Washington. A windy, but sunny day.

Here we are now, sitting on a tree trunk and enjoying the view while "Flowers" quickly disappears in the bushes.

"So stunning this view", I'm whispering as I watch the mountains in the distance we are about to reach in a few days.

"Yes", is your answer lost in thoughts.

"How far do you think it is across the Baltic Sea all the way to Langeland?"

"What?", I'm blanking as you rip me out of my thoughts along the way.

"Once we get back, I want to cross the Baltic Sea by kayak up to Langeland. How long do you think that'll take?", you repeat your question still watching the horizon in the distance.

"You and me? I'm not going! Only if you paddle", I start laughing and turn around facing you.

"That's way too dangerous. Don't you want to grow up already?", am I answering with a smirk.

"No, I do not!", is your reply with a big smile.

"Well, actually you're right, I also don't want us to grow up."

We smile and look deep in our eyes before focusing back on the path's view.

"Flowers" is back from the bushes as she finishes her cigarette, asking to take our picture.

"Nah!", is our simultaneous reply.

Let's get going! Our next goal is the dirt road six miles ahead where there is supposed to be a pit toilet.

Previously, we refilled our water bottles at the piped spring, went for a wee and had a brief chat with the unknown elder man whom we had never met before. The water won't be filtered but supplemented with electrolytes and caffeine. I mean our daily target is 28 miles away.

Once we're at the dirt road and the long-awaited pit toilet, we are welcomed by trail magic. We leave the trail and reach the red car and see that hiker with the big straw hat you and I frequently had seen before. Kif is his name – no trail name available.

There are sausages from the grill, cheese-scalloped bread, pancakes and fruits. Also cookies, chips and coke!

After a while, there is also the guy from the water spring, the Englishman, the diabetic lady that turned a triple crowner with this PCT, an older couple and the girl we had seen in Cascade Locks with her arms full of packages – "Critter".

Then "Flash" and "Raider" are joining in. We're happy to see them but no less disappointed that they were able to catch up so easily and fast.

By now, we've been sitting here for a few hours. The mood is totally chill as Canada is just a stone's throw away. We dig out stories about the Sierra and exchange ideas as how to reach the airport from Manning Park within two weeks. We laugh a lot and have a wonderful time as we know we are at complete ease and will make it on time! No flight will have to be rebooked as we are damn well in time!

I'm daydreaming as I fiddle with my dreads and see you lost in thoughts just as much.

"I think I'll get a tattoo here before we head back", you're talking more to yourself than to me.

"A PCT tattoo?", am I asking.

"Yes, like a souvenir."

"Funny, I've been thinking the same", I'm also still lost in thoughts. "And, what kind of are you considering?"

"There's no way I'm gonna get like the typical one, the logo or mountains that everyone else has. I was thinking to draw a line representing the length of the PCT. Sunk into ink and embracing my leg, displaying the trail."

"Wow, pretty cool.", I'm admitting my admiration from within my daydreams.

"And then it'd be rad to include some knots featuring the individual miles. Something like that, I guess."

Our daily goal gets closer with each hour we're seated. In the beginning it were 17 miles, then 15 and then just 12. Ultimately, we settled for Bear Lake which was some 10 miles ahead. It's five of us now including "Flash", "Raider" and "Flowers".

"Flowers" and "Raider" are challenging each other in their hike and I start to be angry for we did remain seated for quite some time over there causing us do few miles only.

Passing many small lakes, through woods and meadows before arriving at Bear Lake where "Flash", "Raider", "Flowers" and "Critter" are awaiting us already.

"Hi, there you are."

Melanie welcomes us with a radiating smile and presents us tonight's sleeping grounds.

"Just for you guys. I told them you'd have to mount your tent here as it's the biggest one."

We hadn't expected this cordiality and humbly turn our eyes where "Flash" and "Raider" settled for the night – a tiny, inclined spot with roots emerging from the earth.

"All good, we need to wake up pretty early anyway", "Raider" winks at us after sensing our guilty conscience. Thus, we mount our tent and start cooking with Bear Lake's water. It's instant noodles for me and rice for you. We gave the couscous to Melanie. The mood is sublime and in utter ease. "Flowers" and "Flash" are joking around while "Raider" is showing his buggy to you in which after the PCT he'll also go from Mexico all the way to Canada. You're absolutely enchanted by this plan! Of course you were!

In the meantime, I'm busy arranging my dreads after I had thrown a piece of my hair off the Bridge of the Gods into Columbia River. Then, darkness falls and everyone goes to sleep after quickly checking where tomorrow's path will take us.

Just like every night I dig out the diary to put down that day's experiences – the final page.

August 27 of 2019

We're woken up early in the morning by "Critter" who is keen on doing some major miles today. "Flash" and "Raider" want to get up early as well and do shopping at Trout Lake. But "Flash" is still around when our alarm clock rings. He just didn't manage to get up. I look out the tent and see him pack his stuff all relaxed. It is a soothing sight and we stay in bed for a while. But at some point we do get up against our bodies' wills and get our stuff. In the end, we do want to make up some miles from yesterday and possibly even reach 30 miles today.

Teeth are brushed inside the tent again and before we get going, I hop on the "potty" around the corner. We're taking off really chilled and chew on a cereal bar once more.

"Flowers" has the pole position and puts down an enormous velocity that is tough for me to keep with. The distance between us increases and I'm forced to start jogging. At some point I'm out of energy and my shins really start hurting during the descent making me really slow down. You notice it and let me go first so you can keep an eye on me. We catch up with "Flowers" during a peeing break and settle for a slower pace, however want to part ways from the next spring on so everyone is able to walk the ideal speed.

We're having some more peeing breaks, pick mushrooms that we store in our backpacks as we walk in order to not lose time.

"If we meet "Critter" again, I'll confirm if they're edible or not. It would be mushroom soup tonight.", I roll my eyes as I laugh.

At a paved road shortly before Mosquito Creek, we conclude the passage at the trail register and meet the Englishman again and a southbounder.

You and "Flowers" first walk off into different directions and I start filtering the river water. You come back and proudly tell the story of doing business behind that fine spot behind the big trunk.

The usual break begins: Getting out the snacks, splitting them up, eating , drinking lots and then filter some more water to take it with us.

The wind is blowing strongly again and a couple in their 40s walks toward us from the North. As they don't spare a thought to get some water, I'm about to tell them about the scarcity of water for the coming 10 miles before the woman does approach the water source. We get going and quickly stash our spread out stuff that had been blown away with every breeze.

Another hiker comes along, possibly in his 70s. He says he is walking with those two and is about to finish the trail shortly. After all, he does the trail in single parts and has been onto this project for years.

"Twenty-five years back I started hiking parts of the PCT. This time we set off in Trout Lake and hiked towards the next town"

We're quite impressed as he is in an advanced age and appears rather fragile, hobbling around with one very stiff leg. The woman then does carry his water and we decide on shouting at them that there will be no more water until Bear Lake. He calmly states they won't reach that far today anyway.

We're shaking heads at each other before the old man turns around and approaches us again: "We probably won't see each other again..."

"Obviously", am I thinking, "we're venturing northbound and you walk South", before it hits me that he might have said it as he is that old.

"So I will tell you something. I'm an old man. I've lived for many years and experienced a lot. I had hard times in my life and just wanna tell you, no matter what comes, God will be with you. Enjoy every moment of your life. I needed a bad experience to realize that life is short and we should enjoy every second of it. Remember this. And if you come to a point you feel lost pray to God and he will show you the way. God bless you!"

He turns around and disappears in the woods.

The three of us look at each other and also the other two boys that are sitting uphill on a tree smirk.

"Always those Americans and their faith", the three of us agree.

We've been sitting here for an hour and totally got lost in time. I'm asking "Flowers" again to slow down our pace and we decide on the final water break for today. We want to walk another 10 miles and decide on a small creek after White Salmon River.

Shortly after we leave the small wooden bridge, you show us that tree trunk behind which you had found the perfect spot to do business. Melanie and I laugh.

We dig up one topic after the other and Melanie talks about her job in Norway. Reports about her work and how older people are doing over there and that many things are going down way better than in our country.

"Well we're certain we won't ever put our parents into a nursing home", you're interrupting her small monologue. "Yeah, definitely. We want a big place by the lake anyhow."

"With access to the sea!", are you adding with the finger raised as to underline the importance.

"Yes, exactly. So ideally by the Schwentine", I conclude and smile.

"And there has to be a big tree on it. So we better grow it right now so it'll be big when we move there."

"Yeah right. So we'll just creep onto a stranger's property which we believe will be ours in a hundred years and put down the seed or what?"

The three of us crack up.

"Seriously, though. It is in fact the plan to get property soon and build a home piece by piece, with the option of adding some more or building another one next to it. Ideally we'd be getting an old farm but it's not an easy find.", I'm telling and you add: "Yeah something like that so our parents can live with us. My mother has been taking care of the elderly for the past years so it's just natural for us kids to take care of them when the time comes and not some strangers."

"Wow, beautiful idea."

For the first time we're seeing "Flowers" somewhat out of words and with some admiration.

The walking pace increases but it's ok. You slow down on some occasions when discovering some mushrooms here and there, but so far it's just a straight hike and downhill but as of Trout Lake Creek it turns into a steep ascent. That's where "Flowers" steps it up a notch and we're following. But at some point I'm unable to keep up. I let you rush after her as I don't want to stop your own individual journey of building up some solid stamina. Ultimately, we want to run a Marathon six weeks from now.

I fall back and fight my way up. Another mile up before I reach where we planned on meeting again. Half way through I see you waiting for me at a corner until I'm back in your sight. If not in eyesight, then in range of audibility. With a whistle you ensure we're not losing each other – I reconfirm it with whistling back. But this time raising my hiking stick does it. "It's all good, keep walking!"

Once reaching the top, I'm super happy to see you.

"Could we take a short break? Just five minutes?!", I'm gasping for breath.

"Fair enough, five minutes!"

I'm sitting on a massive fallen down trunk and quickly get out a handful of nuts.

"I'll quickly pop the remaining caffeine with the electrolyte water, ok?!", I suggest and you nod with a full mouth.

Seven minutes later and recharged does the way lead us downward only all the way to the break spot.

We're emptying out our trash Ziploc at a trashcan by the FS Road 23. I find a piece of paper nailed to a tree where some phone numbers of trail angels are noted and the hint of having signal to make phone calls a few meters down the road. Across the road and White Salmon River it is in fact another ascent but a swift mile more before we finally reach the creek where we see "Flowers" seated.

"Hi, there you already are.", she smiles and cigarette smoke arises from her mouth.

"I wasn't expecting you guys so fast, I've just gotten here 10 minutes ago."

The smoke slowly passes us and I notice that strong wind from the afternoon has faded.

We're listening to the gurgling sound of the small creek beneath us and don't notice all those fallen trees around us. After all, it is a common sight for this area.

In the middle of this small but trustworthy wooden bridge there is "Flowers" leaning against the wooden handrail. We sit down to her left. Putting down our backpacks next to us and then getting out our snacks. You're sitting there with a rather empty bag of chips and I'm about to interrupt you: "Don't finish the chips.", before you magically cast a new Ziploc filled with Lays Barbecue Chips. The happiness is real. With the chips unfinished, you get up and rush down to refill our water bottles. Back at the bridge, you sit down on the other side. "Don't you want to push something at your back? The wooden bar pressing your back seems so uncomfortable."

"Nah, it's fine, we don't want to stay for too long anyway.", is your response as you filter the water.

"We totally advanced nicely today! It's just 3:30 and we already pushed 20 miles. Perhaps we might get even farther than that spot up the mountain?!", you say full of enthusiasm.

"Yes, that's what I was thinking, too.", Melanie agrees. "For sure we'll have to conquer the ascent, or else we'll be out of water all the way, plus it is another 10 miles", she skeptically adds.

My face reveals some uncertainty as I had been looking forward to an early bed time.

"So have you cried already today?", Melanie mocks me with a massive smirk.

"No", I'm responding, "Not today for a change, but who knows, I might do so later on." I start laughing. We've walked together so much for the past days that she's had the opportunity to witness and share my moods every now and then.

"Sometimes I'm so annoyed by myself that I really don't know how Finni is holding it up with me! But he keeps managing to get me back on track all the time. No idea how, but that's why I love him so much. I'd never be able to tolerate myself!", grateful and ever so in love do I look into your eyes and we wink at each other.

We're sitting there with those delicious snacks in our mouths, laugh and Melanie throws a compliment of her kind: "Well, he is indeed a teddy bear!"

We laugh.

Laughing and crying, screaming and staying quiet, pain and joy, luck and bad luck.

We believe to always be in control of our lives, having it in our hands but at this very moment we realize that this is not the case.

In a blink of an eye our life is directed into other paths.

It is in slow motion, or so it seems, that we see the rotten tree fall toward our direction. So slowly, unreal and millimeter by millimeter it approaches us.

My perception is distorted because today I know in reality it all happened so fast.

Beginning of
Something New

"To love all people unconditionally does not mean to
unconditionally grant them all our time.
Sometimes we can't see someone ever again to truly love him.
That is love as well.
It means granting someone the freedom to exist and to be
happy, even if it has to happen without that person."

- Vironika Tugaleva -

"To unconditionally love means being able to let go and to also
experience love on another level."

- Myself -

It is with deep love that I lay down my head onto your soft, warm belly. Feel my own heart beat pounding in you, displaying a false reality. I'm enjoying this moment and it seems as if time stood still, as if we were given time. Time, we no longer will be given. I close my eyes and take a deep breath, smell the beauty of nature, hear the whooshing sound of the leaves and a blissful smile emerges on my face without noticing it. Grateful for this moment that I am able to live once more, grateful to be able to enjoy and grateful to have you as my boyfriend, my companion and my partner. Grateful for all the love for each other that was there, that is and that will forever remain.

I grab the scissors off the ground that seems so clean, and yet it's covered with earth, leaves and tiny animals crawling around; the ground that has been our home for months and that has grown on us as a sensation of homeland.

I cut off my dearest dreadlock for you, which is right behind my left ear. My dreads, that you've liked so much and that I now knot into your own hair – the hair I loved so much.

It's getting dark slowly and all the helpers are going home. Only Melanie, Philip, Cory and the Sherriff stay.

I'm caressing you in my arms as I sit on the ground of the forest and smell the scent of the trees in a colder turning evening air.

Small lights that turn out to be stars are slowly popping up at the firmament and welcome a peaceful night.

Melanie, Philip and Cory sit down next to us. We're in a circle on the ground – you in the middle of us, in my arms.

In tranquility are we enjoying the silence of the night and a soothing atmosphere embraces us.

I'm protecting your body that I'm keeping tightly attached to me, warming it. I'm picturing you seated in this circle with a smile on your lips.

It is with a wink that you push me to start talking, with my eyes flaring up all in love to you:

"He always laughed and had a smile on his face."

Silence.

I'm hearing myself breathe in and out. My sight wanders off the others into the woods where I sink in the precious memories I henceforth will carry with me.

"He never complained and was always happy! Just a few days ago I asked him if he could complain just one time so I feel better and not be the only one complaining." I smirk and then the others tag along.

Philip's voice cuts the silence of the evening air: "He was so happy out here, loved it and I loved to see him like that."

Yet again, my memories bring forth another smile onto my lips – the thought of you is too beautiful as if I was able to be sad.

The other three folks, too, feel the energy surrounding us from your sheer presence.

"I never met someone like Finn! From the first moment on, I knew he is an awesome guy. Never saw him in a bad mood. Even though we all walked through pouring rain the other day", Philip starts telling. "I'm blessed to have met a person like Finn!"

The others agree nodding.

"I'm thankful to have met Finn eleven years ago and have the honor to be his girlfriend. He taught me so many things and made me the person I am today. He is my soulmate and always will be."

Silence, again, and I'm hearing a bird chirping in the distance, welcoming the awakening of the night. The stars shine brighter and I'm feeling the increasingly chilly night breeze on my skin.

I'm still wearing shorts and a t-shirt as I sit by your side, when Philip squeezes a mat below my butt. Not letting go off you and I'm feeling the warmth reconquer my body when feeling someone putting a jacket around my shoulders.

In love am I arranging the blanket that's warming your body. It's all good, I'm taking care of it.

My thoughts run circles and are fueled with memories falling down onto me like light snow flakes, revealing all those wonderful moments with you.

Quietly, my voice pierces the silence and I'm hearing myself tell stories. Stories, we lived. Stories, you gave me and now enable me to tell them, to carry them out into the world. Stories we wrote and that are worth to be told.

I'm feeling the other three fellas watch me, as they listen carefully and monitor my lips, sucking up those stories become more and more vivid.

I'm hearing a swishing sound, the rustling of the leaves. The sheriff who had been at his car comes back and sits down in our circle with us.

"Did you hear that?", Philip asks the sheriff in complete enthusiasm. "This guy is crazy! He jumped into a river full of crocodiles. This guy lived his life to the fullest!"

Now, Melanie and Cory start telling their stories of meeting you for the first time. How they met and started loving you.

I don't know where this unbelievable energy emerges from, where exactly we – and especially I, myself – source the energy from, with which we make time stand still and virtually consume the moment as we're living it right now. Indeed I don't have the knowledge about the origins of this kind of energy, but a friend of yours told me two weeks later:

"Well it's simple! Finn was full of energy, a man of such strength and power. It's physically just impossible for it to simply vanish. According to the laws of physics, that energy will have to be transferred and I assume it is you where it was transferred to. You carry his power inside of you and pass it on to all of us."

The mortician arrives, the time has come and I am ready.

They give me a moment, I lie down next to you on the forest ground. We're watching the stars in the sky together and I'm quietly humming that song. Singing it for you and a second later it's there: A beautiful, brightly shining shooting star high up above our heads.

I close my eyes, think of you and cast my wish – for you!

I love you!

With a kiss on your forehead I pass you over to the nice fellas dressed in black and watch as they hoist your body into the truck. I'm sensing a smile rush across my lips.

Two days later, I'm on the plane with an empty seat next to me. But I know, as empty as it seems to those around me, it is not. Because you are there, by my side.

Once arriving at home, I'm welcomed by our parents, siblings, families and friends. They've all gathered.

For them, I have brought a piece of your existence back home – and for me, they have brought a piece of your existence to me from within each one of them. The accumulation adds to having you with us very close – and that's what keeps us up.

Here I am now, was never taught to deal with this situation and yet do I sense the intuition as how to handle it.

I greet all those lovely people that are sitting in my parent's garden. Happy to see each and every one of them and as I sit down in their circle, an almost unbearable silence kicks in.

Nobody really knows what to say and thus, I decide to break the silence and start telling. I start reporting on the mountains, the rivers, the snakes and the bears. Describe the pain and the joy and spread the magic that appears to loosen the silence. It is your energy that streams from me in surplus straight through your friends' hearts. I'm sharing the joy with them that we lived over there.

Questions are popping up quickly and as I unpack the backpacks in the middle of the circle, people turn quiet. But it's no silence of uneasiness, however a silence of eagerness to learn about the stories of an unbelievably big adventure.

Grief, solace, laughing and crying – all those are the sensations amongst many others we are confronted with in our minds, whilst trying not to go absolutely crazy. It certainly comes as a true blessing to know we are given an absolutely beautiful circle of friends that in tough times spares no energy to put a hold on everything else and to keep the head high.

No day passes in loneliness. No day where we don't share laughter, no day, where we don't think about you.

It really takes a while for you to arrive and it keeps getting rescheduled.

"Which coffin will Finn be put into by the way?", I'm asking Meike and Birger.

"Yeah, we do have to buy one.", Meike responses pensively.

I'm thinking and know exactly that a coffin will turn out pricey since it should just be the very best for you, while also knowing you wouldn't give a flying one and it might as well be a coffin made of left-over plywood.

"We'll build one!", is my spontaneous suggestion without finalizing this thought.

"Well, I like it.", Meike says and Birger smirks.

Two weeks later, it's done – after endless hours and nights, beautiful and unique just like you.

There you are lying now, in a coffin built by your friends, your brother and your family. With love and utmost precision and without wasting the tiniest thought to the fact that it'll be burned a few days from now. Embedded into a scarf consisting of your friends' shirts who gave you their dearest cloth.

Five days later – the promised festivities. The weather forecast expects a rather rainy day. Bummer, but perhaps we'll be lucky. Or it's just karma, like you'd put it.

For the first time, I'm feeling a little uneasy in my stomach. Is it the excitement for today's day? All those people? The fear to say goodbye although I've already done so. Possibly just the uncertainty of what's next. Indescribable. Jonna stays with me and the two of us drive up to the Rixdorf Manor.

The sun is shining! It's warm!

One cake after another is being arranged. A cake fight is about to happen. With cream, just for you! Because it's supposed to be colorful!

I'm quickly putting on a self-sewn, colored knitted dress, mom's latest knitted socks and my favorite jeans jacket with that nice colorful pattern on the back. Adding Dagmar's chain from Cuba and your watch.

And then it'll be you, or your burned body? Yes! Because you're here! You wouldn't fit into the beautifully decorated urn by Birger. The urn reminds one of Peter Pan and his friends from Neverland, with those three leaves and the colorful paint that lets the wood grain come through.

A boy to never grow up in Neverland! Shooting arrows with his bow at bananas and jumps into the crocodile infested waters in order to flee Captain Hook. Takes off and never loses his smile.

And then they come, the people. To say goodbye – to you.

A long line piles up in front of your guestbook, the family book. All calm and with patience. They've all gathered, for you, and there are more to come. And more. So many! It's touching! It hurts!

I stand at the barn's gate, hidden in the dark. Thinking nobody will see me here. Watching the people arrive and am overwhelmed by the sheer masses.

Then I see Lena and Madeleine appear in the crowd with the whole family. I break down and cry, run into their arms.

The time has come. They sit down and Gerry plays "Halleluja". Tears are shed. Not by me, I'm just enjoying.

The speaker, Mister Knoche, chubby and very likable, starts talking. He tells us a story. Tells greatly about your life and adds my words for you:

Finn lived his life as if there was no tomorrow. Enjoyed every moment of it and enriched that with a big smile. Saw wonders of nature in the tiniest, seemingly invisible detail out there. Showed me that also rainy, stormy days can be a wonderful one if you just go with it.

He impressed me with his way of approaching people completely unprejudiced and open-minded. I admired how he managed to find the right words at the right time to get him exactly where he wanted to be.

He was the only know to know me better than I did myself. Knew how to lure my out of my booth and had me wonder gratefully every single time how it was possible.

His talents, or perhaps just the courage to get his hands on stuff, just to do it without thinking "but what if".

And suddenly, we were spinning like a gear wheel, intertwining into each other, elevating ourselves above and beyond, were radiating with lust of life and ideas as to where leading our journey next up. No adventure appeared too big, no path too long, no ocean too deep and no mountain too high. We planned our journeys with the following one in mind already. Nobody could stop us. One stunning sensation!

And so he ventures forth, with a backpack loaded with great plans to never run out of!

I'm so grateful from the deepest of my heart that you made me the person I now am. Standing here and now, full of energy and confidence and the certainly you'll never take your eyes off me.

I'll love you forever.

Your Larry – TT :-*

Gerry plays another song and then it's Offi. He unexpectedly gets out his trumpet and starts playing. Playing for you! Mind-blowing! I'm so proud!

We walk to the front. First Meike and Birger, then I. A kiss on this enchanting urn – thank you Birger. I smile and walk off. Passing all those people. They're watching, I'm not.

"Do I have to hug everyone now?", am I asking Birger.

"You don't have to if you don't want to!"

No, I do not. Not here. Not because a norm asks me to! I turn around and browse. For whom? I don't know. And then it started. People come to you and hug you. They keep saying "My condolences." I don't get it. What's that supposed to mean? Why are they saying it? Kamila stands in front of me and says: "I love you!" So beautiful! Different and honest. Thank you, Kamila!

I start approaching people myself, taking control of the situation and deciding myself whom to hug. Many of your study boys like Dardan and Malte amongst others found it hard to come. It felt good being able to do something for them and hugging them. Not being the one that's being hugged.

It's time to get you to your tree. To drive in the Landcruiser – your car! An Australian Landcruiser with a right-hand drive and a snorkel we missed to badly back in the Outback at our Holden Jackaroo. With a V8 making some solid noise in the gateway.

Once at the woodland burial site are we to embed your urn into the earth. Birger and I lower it carefully. Meike, Birger, Leif, Helen, Jonna, aunt Elke, uncle Helge, Tina, Norman, Offi, Lisa, Andreas and I speak some words to you. Everyone for him- and herself and with a hand full of earth to it. Jonna, Leif, Andreas and I take the sand. Release it into the hole. Cover your urn with earth until the hole is covered. We're laying out the flowers around it in a circle. Beautiful!

There we are now, in silence. And then Offi takes his trumpet and plays. Plays for you, his big brother.

There he stands now, your tree. That copper beech enlightened by the sun peeking through the leaves. The wind lets the leaves rustle and somewhere up in the crowns two birds of prey tell us how great they're doing.

After a cake feast, we leave Rixdorf Manor and drive back to Schellhorn. Prior to that, a brief visit with Mirko, Svenja, Marleen and Maja at yours.

Back home the party is on! No minute passes without: "... and another one for Finn!", and the later it gets, the more beer is spilled every time we toast. We're laughing: "Finni will get real drunk!" We drink, smoke and cheer. Mirko gathers everyone. The group should not split into two groups! We toast at the beer table:

"The music is long gone, the band is home already.
It's just me left with a few friends, a few beers.
It's drinking and laughing and telling stories all night long
and I lean back and enjoy my happiness in silence.
Those are the moments I wish
would never come to an end.

Dear good old times, stand still for a while,
take a rest as it's so wonderful right now.
Let's stay here and today and put all watches to a hold
we want this moment to last 100 years.

We haven't seen each other for a while, almost half a year
we needed time and the distance and now it's back
with a suitcase in one hand and a smile on the face
and I embrace it in my arms and hold it real tight.

Dear good old times, stand still for a while,
take a rest as it's so wonderful right now.
Let's stay here and today and put all watches to a hold
we want this moment to last 100 years.

An unexpected reunion, a smile as you walk by,
a solved argument, a conquered disease.
Some wonderful news, scoring even in the additional time,
so many moments rush by way too quickly.

Dear good old times, stand still for a while,
take a rest as it's so wonderful right now.
Let's stay here and today and put all watches to a hold
we want this moment to last 100 years."

- Song 'Time, stand still!' by Dritte Wahl -

The table shakes, everyone yells and the beer is flowing ... into the mouth and across the whole table. We're laughing and crying. Hug each other and dance.

In the middle of the night, Meike wakes up. There was a huge bang.
- The bees! -
The table with the beehive on it collapsed.
- Finn -
A sign that you enjoyed the night as much as we did.

"It's kinda weird! We're back in Germany now but life as usual just goes on", were your thoughts after we came back from India. Gotten the realization that life goes on either way, wherever you are.

I had to leave the PCT but got you got carried along by those people we were able to meet. "Raider" who awarded you that name took your cap, "Flash" took my dirtiest Ziploc all the way up to the Canadian border.

14 September of 2019, the day you and I wanted to be up the monument with beer in our hands, those two made it up and finished the hike for you.

A whole bunch of beautiful deeds happened to properly honor you, Finn Bastian.

You received the award to have walked the whole PCT. Hikers, companions – friends put down flowers, letters, images, beers and a monument for "Colors" at that bridge.

And in Cascade Locks they celebrated it – your life!

Epilogue

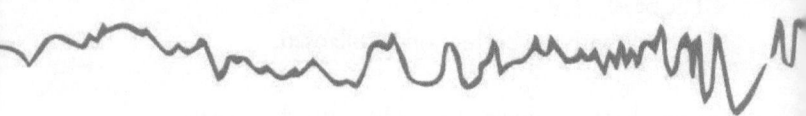

Hikerlegs · Yearning · Grief · Love

"Mountains are quiet masters and draw reticent students."

- Johann Wolfgang von Goethe -

How do people handle the change to be back in civilization from one moment to another? What kind of emotions emerge and which memories tear you out your daily hustle? When do we start yearning to be back on our feet and where does the next journey take us to? Who poses the questions and why didn't we just stay there?

We've started to smell the surroundings more intensively. Noticed sounds subconsciously, saw stunning landscapes and watched fascinating fauna.

Walked, starved, had little energy team up with pure lust of life and happiness that flared up every single time we had a great view and fell asleep under millions of stars.

And then you're back. Surrounded by cars, people, a surplus of groceries, kitchens where you can cook, drinkable water wherever you look, a warm shower every day and a comfortable bed. A roof above your head and suddenly the weather doesn't matter anymore. The silence in a room drives you nuts and so do all those tons of people. The movie on TV totally wears you out and you go to bed all exhausted. You kneel down to tie your shoes ... and then they get to you ... the images. They strike you like a lightning. You're back on the trail. Remember it. It's just fragments – but they're clear.

The next time you kneel down ... whoosh ... and again, you're back on the trail for a brief moment.

You drink or eat, take a bath or just lie down in the grass, listen to music or are not doing anything major and yet every time the images hit you without being able to control it. Sometimes nice moments and sometimes exhausting or sad memories. They come as quickly as they fade away. If you like you can remain within or you push them away.

I pushed them away. Wasn't able to bear those images yet. Couldn't stand to have you around me just to realize you're gone.

It still hurts but I know it'll be beautiful at some point. I'll be able to remain in these thoughts and reminisce our amazing time with a smile on my face and read this book's lines for the 97th time.

One changes. Thinks, feels, acts and lives different. Prioritizes in a different way and has a new, more relaxed way of looking at things.

However, often times I wondered whether it's really just the experiences and memories on the trail or whether it was your death that changed me so much without noticing it. Can a person change within minutes? Adjust the way of thinking so much and drive the actions to different paths?

Ultimately, I concluded it was a little bit of both. The way together with you had prepared me for the finale. Made me stronger – or simply free. To be living here and now, carrying along the past's experiences in order to smile as I look to the future.

Although time heals all wounds, time is indeed a relative matter and is being experienced differently by everyone and increases with the intensity of the actions.

The time with you was, is and will remain intense, amazing, meaningful and in every aspect beautiful. And you have no idea how much I miss the time with you. How much I miss you. Again and again hope arises that I was just dreaming, that you'll come around the corner and I'd be mute in all the happiness to be seeing you again. That it was just a terrible nightmare. One of those I frequently had and where you'd be lying next to me each time I wake up from them. And you'd calm me down in love: "Oh sugar, that was just a terrible dream, I'm here for you!"

There is this imagination that if only I wish for it strongly enough I might encounter the possibility to bring you back.

Where I'd close my eyes and simply think of it hard enough. Wishing a small fairy or the ability to turn in everything just to be hugging you once more. Being able to look into your beautiful brown eyes again and tell you: "I love you!"

Unable to grasp the inability to ever hold you again, to give you a kiss on the lips, to brush through your hair and lie down my head onto your chest. Your scent, your voice, your smile, your warmth and your heart beat turn into eternal memories now.

But I don't want to make lots of space for grief and yearning – however, it does do well to you to do justice to these sentiments. Embracing them for a brief moment before putting them aside with care. Shifting the focus from sorrow toward the magical wonders awaiting us everywhere and displaying dimensions of our life we had only known within the term of love.

"There is an extremely strong force for which science has yet to discover a formula. It is a force to contain all others, to regulate them and to even be found around each phenomenon to be active in the universe without being identified by us yet. This universal force is LOVE.

Whenever scientists are browsing for a universal theory, they've always forgotten this invisible and most powerful of all forces.

Love is light, as it enlightens the receiver as well the sender. Love is gravity, because it makes some people feel attracted to others. Love is power, because it multiplies the best we have, and allows humanity not to be extinguished in their blind selfishness. Love unfolds and reveals. For love we live and die. Love is God and God is Love.

This force explains everything and gives meaning to life. This is the variable that we have ignored for too long, maybe because we are afraid of love because it is the only energy in the universe that man has not learned to drive at will. To give visibility to love, I made a simple substitution in my most famous equation. If instead of $E=mc2$, we accept that the energy to heal the world can be obtained through love multiplied by the speed of light squared, we arrive at the conclusion that love is the most powerful force there is, because it has no limits.

After the failure of humanity in the use and control of the other forces of the universe that have turned against us, it is urgent that we nourish ourselves with another kind of energy. If we want our species to survive, if we are to find meaning in life, if we want to save the world and every sentient being that inhabits it, love is the one and only answer.

Perhaps we are not yet ready to make a bomb of love, a device powerful enough to entirely destroy the hate, selfishness and greed that devastate the planet. However, each individual carries within them a small but powerful generator of love whose energy is waiting to be released.

When we learn to give and receive this universal energy,
dear Lieserl, we will have affirmed that love conquers all,
is able to transcend everything and anything, because
love is the quintessence of life."

-Albert Einstein, Loveletter to his daughter-

All these "things" I'm living, all these moments in which I sense you, knowing you're there, all these signs you're giving me and all the love you once gave me and I'm still feeling to this day, deliver the certainty to me that we are still together every day. But there have been moments of doubt, when I couldn't fully believe. I was forced too much into the boundaries of society, secretly waiting for another sign from you.

But as I listened to those lines for the first time today, I smiled and equally teared up, because there was the response, the confirmation of my belief. The confirmation that our unconditional love we had given each other and still are giving each other eventually is capable of holding it up and is mightier than everything else in this world. That the love for each other is an invisible ribbon to connect us – in spite of death having reaped your earthly existence off this planet. I feel your love at all times and feel secure and protected. Feel your power in me and how it guides me.

It shall no longer be mine to feel your body as such, to hear your voice and laughter. To smell you and look into your beautiful eyes. To kiss your lips and feel your moustache tingle my nose. To lie in your arms and listen to your cheering words.

But what is left to me exceeds all senses us living creatures are given – that's love. The love to have united us. The love to have made tough times a little easier. The love that turned every compromise and every favor we'd do for each other into a present of love for the other.

I still carry your love inside as much as you carry mine inside of you, and that, forever. There is no end to it. Our love story is eternal. Invincible for all eternity.

- No matter where. -

PCT Glossary

AS [Ant Street]

This was a short, self-made term letting the other one know about an ant street to cross our way.

Bear Box

Lockable boxes for food you can usually find at official camp grounds in order to keep bears off people's food. They also contain tooth paste, creams of any kind and cooking utensils.

Bear Can

This just like bear boxes serves to keep bears off our food. Usually round like a barrel, weighs around 1.2kg and is being carried in or on the backpack. A thought-out system allows the lid to be opened merely with finesse – which turns out tough on Homo Sapiens in icy temperatures.

Bonus Miles

Whenever you roam off the trail toward sources or any sort of supplying spots, you chalk those miles off as bonus miles as they are no official PCT miles. Also those typical additional miles when wandering around through the Sierra in a slight loss of orientation.

Bounce Box

A supply box that's kept being sent to my future self. Contains amongst other stuff medication, stuff we'll later on need or not anymore. On top of that, items you find on your way and don't want to carry along but do want to take home later on like for instance a small tent peg collection.

Bubble

A Bubble full of hikers. Crammed and bundled as they take off at the same time into the same direction. Usually to be found shortly ahead of entering the High Sierra Nevada when the best possible snow conditions make people hike. We were always ahead of that herd which made us feel like pioneers of ice. Which lea us to making those unsolicited bonus miles, though.

Cache

A small spot of water, often times in the desert, at the side of a small dirt road. This is being refilled by volunteers of the PCT. However, this cannot be planned for as a stable water source.

Camel Up

You could saddle some camels, but it's easier to cover your water need straight at the water spot yourself. Which is where you drink as much as possible to avoid carrying surplus kilos. This excludes the water supply at the water caches. You'll only take as much as necessary!

Camp Spot

This describes the place where you'll mount your tent for the night, ideally somewhat even grounds with roots coming through and mostly rock hard. Possible camp spots include: Forests, meadows, rocks, lava stones, snow, the backyard of a trail angel and even the inners of classic American diners. Important here, always at least 200 ft from any water source.

Cat Hole

A hole at least 6-8 inches (15-20cm) deep in which you'll defecate when required. When not required, no hole necessary. That holey is exclusively meant for excrement. The toilet paper will be dragged along safely stored in a sealable bag for the entire stretch or until you reach a trashcan. Also in this case: 200 feet to water and sleeping grounds.

Cowboy Camping

Rattle snakes, scorpions and especially mosquitos are your best friends for the night. Without a tent, tarp or a mosquito net your night will turn into a no-risk-no-fun adventure.

Day Hiker

A hiker who is on the move at the PCT but is just up for a day's excursion. Usually a rather rare sight.

Dry Camping

Whenever there won't be water sources up next, you'll refill as much water as possible ahead of it in order to have sufficient supplies to cover drinking, cooking, brushing teeth until the next morning. You'd be cooking and eating at one of those places and do more miles afterwards before mounting your tent. This camping style is particularly suitable in areas with bears around as to avoid attracting them.

Flip Flop

Skipping parts of the trail, entering at a different spot just to hike the skipped part at a later point in time. This often times was done in the Sierra area as 2019 showed a 200-300% increase of snow to regular years.

Glissade

More or less exciting downhills at the backside of the passes. Happens merely in plain laziness that you rush down on the icy backs in your way too short pants.

Hero

A brief stop at a place that you'll leave the same day you entered. You might as well call it a pit stop.

Hiker Box

A box in which a hiker will place and donate unwanted food or equipment. Those boxes can usually be found in hostels, supermarkets and at frequented spots.

Hiker Hunger

A type of hunger that's largely eradicated in our Western society. Certainly not comparable to the hunger our grandparents were forced to live with in war times, however.

Hiker Legs

About one or two months in, your legs are used to the daily drill and you can easily call them hiker legs.

Hiker Midnight

It's lights out by 9pm the latest.

Hiker Porn

An entertainment program instituted by nature that's G rated. This unofficial term was brought to life when we witnessed an avalanche right in front of us.

Hiker Trash

The state of a hiker he'll find himself in after days of hiking, sweating and without access or interest in bodily hygiene. In town, it may lead to confusions with homeless people.

HYOH

Hike your own hike.

JMT [John Muir Trail]

This trail leads from Yosemite National Park all the way to Mount Whitney. It covers some areas of the PCT and most hikers will do this one southbound, making you encounter many JMTs on your way through the Sierra.

LNT

Leave no trace. The most important rule on the trail! Don't leave any traces except for your footprint.

Nero [Nearly a Zero]

A day you make just a few miles, way less than on your average schedule.

NoBo [North Bounder]

A northbound-hiking person. We were NoBos.

Night Hike

This can come in handy to escape the desert's heat or to make up some miles.

Poop Kit

An assortment of a shovel, unused toilet paper, and if it's not very first day, used toilet paper – which should be sealed off in a bag.

Postholing

Those mean unforeseeable holes that occur when walking through snow and you sink in deep. You may break your leg easily and end up looking like a post piercing through the snow. Painful, energy-sucking but usually avoidable by daring to walk across the snow layer in the early hours.

Puffy

An ultra-light and foldable duvet jacket, alternatively with a synthetic filling. Just has to be warm.

Resupply Box

Supply in the shape of food. This kind of supply saves you the effort of passing a town and enables you to do more miles. These will be packed ahead and be sent to your future self just like bounce boxes. The tricky thing is anticipating your own taste as it'll drastically change over the weeks of popping the same grub for days.

Ridge

I'm assuming some 80% of the trail are walked along the mountain ridge. You'll conquer vertigo and be able to enjoy the view.

Section Hiker

A section hiker will only hike the PCT stretch by stretch. This bears the advantage of choosing the ideal timing. Possible to avoid mosquito wars in Oregon and crossing passes without tons of merciless snow.

Skipping

Just like flip flop, this means leaving out certain parts of the trail, however, without the intention of doing them later on.

Slack Packing

Catching up on stretches of the PCT without or with little luggage. This is how we made up 8 miles on day 53 at Tehachapi.

SoBo [South Bounder]

A southbound-hiking person.

Sun Cups

Also egg carton. Because the sun-shaped snow holes resemble either one. A slippery structure where the challenge is to not break a leg and advancing at snail pace.

Thru Hike / - Hiker

The hiking of a long distance hike like the PCT, AT or CDT within one year or season, respectively.

Town Gravity

The amenities of a town will almost make you forget the beauty of nature. Fortunately, there is trail gravity, too, calling you as soon as you spend too much time in the chaos of civilization.

TP [Toilet Paper]

Self-explanatory, but it took me a while before realizing people weren't talking about teepees whenever they were about to do business.

Trailangel

Trail angels are the ambassadors of trail magic. Whether it's sandwiches by the road, a hitch to town, a roof above your head or a can of coke, they'll deliver happiness with a smile straight to the hikers' hearts and will only ask donations, if anything at all.

Trail Family

This term by no means exaggerates. It is a family and the term perfectly gathers the incredible sense of community we're living; and we yet have to find outside of said family.

Trailmagic

Stuff we'll pay little attention to in "normal" life.

Trailname

A nickname you'll be awarded by others during the hike. No limitations for this one.

Trail Register

Logbooks or simply a few sheets on top of a peak that hold the hikers' names who passed through. Quite useful things enabling to see who and when someone from your trail family came through and whether the attempt of catching up is worth it.

Triple Crown

Someone who mastered all three big ones: PCT (Pacific Crest Trail), AT (Appalachian Trail) and the CDT (Continental Divide Trail).

Zero

A day where you'll chalk off zero miles on the PCT. This serves as recreation and especially resupply in town. Our last zero was in South Lake Tahoe, from where it were 48 days and 1.800 kilometers without a break.

End

Off to the next adventure!

Acknowledgement

I would like to thank all my friends who supported me in the creation and realization of this book and who took the time to read my manuscript:
Bettina Reichard, Dr. Kirsten Böttcher, Mona Peters, Nele Päplow and Lena Utermann.

Special thanks to all the donors who helped me get this book translated into English: Tina, Lena, Liz and Marcin, Lori, Nane, Kai, Marvin, Kris, the Fren-Family, "Sky Howie", Birte , Janna Marie, Doris and of course Sebastian Henrich, who immediately took the time to do the translation.

And I would like to thank my family and friends, who have accompanied and supported me in every situation. Never lost sight of me and always encouraged me.

However, my greatest thanks goes to you, Finn, who managed to make me the person I am today and who guided me in the evening hours in which I wrote this book.

Larissa Stawicki
Finn Bastian

We lived our lives like there was no tomorrow, but with a backpack full of plans that would never have been empty.

No adventure too big, no way too far, no sea too deep and no mountain too high.

We learned to love life, we - Finn and Larissa, a couple since youth and inseparable from then on. As an aspiring civil engineer and architect far from writing, life brought us to this book.

www.dirty-colors.com

abenteuer_gefunden